A Disciple's Path

Deepening Your Relationship with Christ and the Church

Daily Workbook

James A. Harnish with Justin LaRosa

Abingdon Press
Nashville

A DISCIPLE'S PATH DAILY WORKBOOK

First edition published as ISBN 978-1-4267-43498.
ISBN 978-1-5018-58123. New cover printing with minor revisions, 2018.

(New cover printing with minor revisions)
18 19 20 21 22 23 24 25 26 27—10 9 8 7 6 5 4 3 2 1
MANUFACTURED IN THE UNITED STATES OF AMERICA

ACKNOWLEDGMENTS

With appreciation to Rachel Burns, who led the team at Hyde Park United Methodist Church that developed the "Discipleship Pathway," which formed the basis for *A Disciple's Path*. She not only helped design the path; she walks it.

CONTENTS

Introduction: "Follow Me!"

"Follow me!" The invitation is so simple a small child can understand it. When it was time for my preschool-age grandchildren to come to dinner, pick up their toys, or head to the bathtub, I used to say, "Follow me!" and start marching down the hall like the drum major in a parade. It meant that it was time to get up and move! And it worked. They would get up and join the parade.

"Follow me!" is the invitation with which Jesus called his first disciples. It appears twenty-one times in Matthew, Mark, Luke, and John. Every time he says it, Jesus is calling for decisive action. He invites and expects a response.

Peter, James, and John drop their fishing nets to fish for people. Matthew leaves his tax-collector table and ends up with his name on a Gospel. The rich young ruler hears the invitation but sadly walks away.

As Jesus' path leads closer to the cross, the invitation becomes more costly. He lets the disciples know that following him will mean taking up a cross.

Then, at the empty tomb, the women hear the angel say that the risen Christ is already out ahead of them, calling them to follow him into a new life. In John's Gospel, Jesus' final word to Peter is, "Follow me."

And now, the invitation comes to you!

Wherever you are in your faith journey, this is your invitation to follow Jesus too. You are invited to take your next step along the path of discipleship leading to a life that fulfills Jesus' great commandment that we love God with all our hearts, souls, minds, and strength and love others as we have been loved by God.

Deciding to follow Jesus and take the next step along the discipleship pathway raises several important questions:

- What does it mean to follow Jesus? And what does it mean to be a follower of Jesus in the Methodist tradition?

- What are the specific practices that will help you grow into the likeness of Christ and become a part of God's transformation of the world?

- How can you discover your unique gifts and become engaged in transforming ministry in the world, and what role does the church play in this process?

Our Wesleyan heritage responds to these questions in two ways:

1. We believe that every follower of Jesus is involved in an ongoing process of transformation made possible by God's grace.

This means that we don't just "get saved" and wait to go to heaven. God's love and grace are continually at work within us "until all of us come to the unity of the faith and of the knowledge of the Son of God, to maturity, to the measure of the full stature of Christ" (Ephesians 4:13).

God's grace is a central theme of the Wesleyan tradition. It describes the undeserved, unearned love of God that meets us where we are but loves us too much to leave us there. God's grace begins its work in our lives before we respond in commitment to Christ and continues God's work within us throughout our lives. Charles Wesley described this continual growth in grace when he taught Methodists to sing,

> *Changed from glory into glory,*
> *till in heaven we take our place,*
> *till we cast our crowns before thee,*
> *lost in wonder, love, and praise.*[1]

2. We follow practical methods or disciplines to grow in the love of God.

John Wesley was not only a theologian and preacher; he was also a pragmatic leader who organized his followers around specific disciplines by which "the people called Methodists" would continue to grow in the love of God. It's in our Methodist DNA to design practical methods by which the love and grace of God become tangible realities that transform the way we live.

The label "Methodist" was mockingly applied to the members of the Holy Club at Oxford because they were so methodical in the development of their spiritual lives and in their service to the needs of people around them. These disciplines were practiced primarily in small groups that were designed for biblical study, spiritual growth, compassionate service, and mutual accountability. These same methods of spiritual discipline continue to be the source of vitality and spiritual growth wherever the Methodist movement is alive and well in this world.

A Disciple's Path

A Disciple's Path will guide you in the practical application of these two ideas and will help you understand God's role, your role, and the church's role in the process of discipleship. It combines a uniquely Wesleyan understanding of growth in grace with the time-tested practices of spiritual discipline expressed in the vows of membership[2] when we commit ourselves to be involved in the church and support its ministries through our

> **prayers**
> **presence**
> **gifts**
> **service**
> **witness**

Because we practice these disciplines in Christian community with other disciples who are walking the same path, *A Disciple's Path* is designed to be used in a group, such as in a new member orientation class, an ongoing class or small group, or even a congregation-wide emphasis. However you use it, two resources will guide you along your journey.

Daily Workbook

Because we learn best by doing, the *Daily Workbook* engages you in reflection on Scripture and teaching material, including questions for response, and guides you in practicing the discipline for the week. Five reflections are provided for each week (each requiring less than thirty minutes). Each reflection includes Scripture, a message for the day, personal reflection questions and prompts with space

for writing, and a prayer (not always in this order). These reflections become the basis of the discussion, sharing, and accountability in the group session. In this way, the workbook will help you develop your own pattern of spiritual discipline.

Companion Reader

The *Companion Reader* provides important biblical and theological insights and background material on each week's theme from a distinctively Wesleyan perspective. It may be used by both participants and leaders to enhance understanding of the spiritual disciplines, find answers to questions, and promote deeper reflection.

These two books and the accompanying DVD and leader resources grew out of the life and practice of disciples just like you who were searching for the most effective way to respond to Jesus' invitation to follow him. Our prayer is that they will help you follow him too.

"I am not afraid that the people called Methodists should ever cease to exist either in Europe or America. But I am afraid, lest they should only exist as a dead sect, having the form of religion without the power. And this undoubtedly will be the case, unless they hold fast both the doctrine, spirit, and discipline with which they first set out."
—John Wesley[3]

What Does It Mean to Be a United Methodist?

A Brief History

Methodism began as an eighteenth-century spiritual renewal movement within the Church of England. John Wesley, a priest in the Church of England, and his brother Charles, a priest and songwriter, are most often identified as the founders of the movement, although neither intended to start a new church.

The Wesleys emphasized scriptural holiness, vital piety, and acts of justice and compassion. Observers derided the Wesleys and their followers for being so "methodical" in their discipline and spiritual practice. The Wesleys embraced this description as their moniker, and the Methodist movement was born.

Once the movement crossed the ocean to colonial America, it took on a life of its own, becoming The Methodist Episcopal Church in 1784. Eventually, the Wesleys' governing authority waned over the American Methodists, even though their spiritual and doctrinal influence remained.

In the nineteenth century, the growth of The Methodist Episcopal Church paralleled the emergence of another Christian movement in the United States, The Evangelical United Brethren Church. The EUB Church was born from a merger of The Evangelical Church and The United Brethren Church, with strong roots in the Midwest and the Northeast. Over time, the Methodist and EUB churches recognized their similarities in doctrine, practice, and church organization. In 1968, these churches became The United Methodist Church.

About The United Methodist Church

Structure:

Like the United States government, The United Methodist Church is made up of three branches: executive, legislative, and judicial. The United Methodist Church's version of these three is the Council of Bishops, the General Conference, and the Judicial Council.

Every United Methodist congregation is connected with every other United Methodist congregation around the world. This connection impacts everything from the way pastors are appointed to the way we fulfill our mission around the globe.

The connectional system begins with the local church and extends to the annual local church charge conference (which elects representatives and guides a congregation in fulfilling its mission), to districts, to annual conferences (where an assigned bishop announces ministerial appointments for the year), to jurisdictions (five in the United States) and central conferences (outside the United States), and finally to the General Conference. The General Conference, which meets once every four years, is made up of laypeople and clergy elected by their annual conferences. Its main purpose is to vote on church law. If enacted by the General Conference, the proposed laws are published in *The United Methodist Book of Discipline.*

Key Beliefs and Values:
- We believe that salvation is found in and through Jesus Christ.

- We believe that the Bible is the word of God and the primary authority for Christian life and faith. While we believe the Bible is true, we do not believe every verse of the Bible must be interpreted literally. Methodists interpret Scripture through reason, tradition, and experience.
- We believe in justification by grace through faith.
- We believe in personal holiness and social action.
- We believe in living by grace and striving for holiness—to become like Christ.
- We believe in the balance of heart and head.
- We believe in providence on the one hand and human freedom on the other.
- We value tradition and are willing to embrace change.
- We believe that God's redemptive love is realized in human life by the activity of the Holy Spirit.
- We believe that we are part of Christ's universal church as we become conformed to Christ.
- We recognize the kingdom of God as both a present and a future reality.
- While affirming the faith we share in common with all other Christians, we also affirm the unique emphasis the Wesleyan tradition places on the love and grace of God.
- We believe the sacraments of baptism and Holy Communion are means by which the intangible reality of God's grace touches our lives in tangible ways.
- The mission of The United Methodist Church is "to make disciples of Jesus Christ for the transformation of the world."

Frequently Asked Questions

1. Is there anything unique about United Methodist doctrine?

United Methodists place a strong emphasis on God's grace as an active part of every human's life from the moment of birth (*prevenient grace*), to the individual's saving experience of God through Jesus Christ (*justifying grace*), and throughout the rest of his or her life in Christian discipleship (*sanctifying grace*). These stages of grace serve as the critical foundation for other important Methodist distinctions, such as beliefs in human free will and infant baptism.

In addition, United Methodist doctrine affirms the Quadrilateral, a unique fourfold formula for discerning God's purpose and activity in the world. Chief among the components is Scripture, which attests to the nature and work of God and is our principal authority, interpreted through tradition (the collection of Christian witness throughout the centuries), experience (the encounter of the Holy Spirit in contemporary events), and reason (the capacity of intellect and rationale). The convergence of these elements guides United Methodists in discussing important matters of biblical, doctrinal, and social concern.

2. What do United Methodists believe about God and the Bible?

United Methodist beliefs share much in common with other mainline Protestant denominations. We believe in a trinitarian God in keeping with Christian tradition. This means that we believe in one God made known to us as Father, Son, and Holy Spirit. The Father, or God Almighty, is the creative God who authored all life. The Son is the redeeming God who became fully human—Jesus Christ. The Holy Spirit is the sustaining God who nurtures individuals and communities.

We believe that as God's creations, we are meant to live in a holy covenant with this trinitarian God. However, we also teach that we have broken this covenant by our sins, and we are forgiven by God's love and saving grace in Jesus Christ. We believe that Jesus was God on earth (the product of a virgin conception) in the form of a man who was crucified for the sins of all people, and who was physically resurrected to bring us the hope of eternal life.

Other beliefs we share with other Christian churches include the following:

- The grace of God is perceived by people through the work of the Holy Spirit in their lives and in their world.
- We are part of a universal church and must work with all Christians to spread the love of God.
- Close adherence to the teachings of Scripture is essential to the faith because Scripture is the word of God.

United Methodists uphold the Bible as the primary witness of the nature and activity of God and God's relationship to humanity. Our canon, or official collection of biblical material, is the same as other Protestant churches—sixty-six books (thirty-nine in the Old Testament, twenty-seven in the New Testament).

3. What do United Methodists believe about social issues? What are the United Methodist Social Principles?

The United Methodist Church puts a great emphasis on service to others, outreach, and evangelism as the expressions of God's love at work in the world. We have a strong legacy in ministries of mercy and justice. John Wesley gave the early Methodists three guiding principles for their lives, which he called "General Rules":

- Do no harm by avoiding evil.
- Do good in every possible way.
- Be faithful in the practices of Christian discipline.[1]

Methodist hospitals, schools, relief agencies, and numerous other organizations seek to alleviate human suffering, promote peace and justice, and improve the welfare of the global community. For more information about how The United Methodist Church is involved in missions around the world, see the website of the General Board of Global Ministries (www.umcmission.org).

The Social Principles is the document that best reflects the ongoing dialogue within the United Methodist community in matters of social, economic, and political importance. The Social Principles is an expression of the church's effort to discern biblically, traditionally, experientially, and rationally the Methodist stance on the controversial issues of the day. To find more information and to read the full text of the Social Principles, visit www.umc.org.

4. Do I have to be a United Methodist in order to receive Communion?

No. United Methodists observe an open invitation for Communion, which means one need not be a member of a United Methodist congregation in order to observe the Eucharist. The only requirement is a personal desire to experience the grace of God revealed through Jesus Christ. Methodists believe that Holy Communion celebrates the grace of God that is present with us as we share in the body (the bread) and the blood (grape juice) of Christ.

Often parents wonder whether it is appropriate for their children to receive Communion. Since there is no official doctrine on the matter, parents are free to decide at what point their children are able to understand its meaning and significance, and we welcome children of any age to receive the sacrament.

5. What do United Methodists believe about baptism?

We believe that baptism is the sign of the grace of God that claims us as God's own children. We believe it is the beginning point of our spiritual journey. Baptism is the outward and visible sign of the inward and spiritual grace of God's work of love in an individual's life even before he or she is able to understand it or choose to accept it. Methodists call this "prevenient grace." While some denominations choose to wait until a person is able to couple baptism with understanding and public profession of faith, we invite the parents and the church to affirm this grace on behalf of the child as they pledge to raise the child in the faith until the time that the child is able to accept God's grace for himself or herself, usually at the time of confirmation, which is between sixth and eighth grades in most churches. Methodists practice baptism by sprinkling, pouring, or immersion.

6. Does The United Methodist Church have a pope, president, or leader of all Methodists?

No one person speaks on behalf of all United Methodists. Because the movement was born in America during British colonialism, the first Methodists in the country sought to avoid a church governing structure that resembled a monarchical system. From the local congregation to the denominational level, important decisions are made by a coordination of shared power. The General Conference is a gathering of nearly one thousand delegates equally divided between laypeople and clergy. It provides the missional, organizational, budgetary, and doctrinal direction for the whole church. The Social Principles, referenced previously, is a product of this dialogue.

7. What are the membership vows of The United Methodist Church, and what do they include?

The membership vows are grouped into three categories: (1) profession of faith in Jesus Christ to become part of Christ's universal church, (2) declaration of loyalty to The United Methodist Church in particular, and (3) a pledge to participate faithfully in this local congregation through prayers, presence, gifts, service, and witness.

The vow to support the church through prayers, presence, gifts, service, and witness is not a multiple-choice vow. Just as Jesus calls us to love God and neighbor through heart, soul, mind, and strength, so being a disciple involves the whole self; we strive to commit our entire lives to God.

For more information about what United Methodists believe, visit www.umc.org or www.umcdiscipleship.org.

WEEK 1
A DISCIPLE'S PATH DEFINED

When was the last time you watched a toddler learning to walk? There's always a lot of stumbling, falling down, getting up, falling again, and then taking off in a burst of energy and running straight into the sofa. There's also a lot of hand holding and support from parents and grandparents along the way. But as children continue to grow, they get better at walking, and they keep walking for the rest of their lives.

There is a lot of walking in the Bible, and it's more than just getting from one place to another. Throughout Scripture—from God walking with Adam and Eve in the garden of Eden in Genesis to the risen Christ walking among the churches in the book of Revelation—walking is the basic biblical metaphor for living and growing in relationship with God.

The psalmist said, "Your word is a lamp to my feet and a light to my path" (Psalm 119:105). When Jesus called his first disciples, they got up, left their past behind, and walked along with him. The writer of the epistles named for John wrote, "Whoever says, 'I abide in him,' ought to walk just as he walked" (1 John 2:6) and "This is love, that we walk according to his commandments. . . . You must walk in it"

(2 John 1:6). An old gospel hymn says, "When we walk with the Lord in the light of his word, what a glory he sheds on our way!"[1]

Discipleship is all about learning to walk with Christ. We stumble. We fall. We pick ourselves up and go again. We are surrounded by a community of disciples who pick us up, hold our hands, and keep walking with us along the way. But we keep on walking. We keep on growing. We keep moving into a life that is more and more deeply centered in loving God with our whole heart, mind, soul, and strength. We keep on loving others the way we have been loved by God. Spiritual growth is the process by which we grow into the likeness of Jesus Christ, but only if we keep on walking with him.

You have accepted the invitation to follow Jesus and take the next step along the pathway of discipleship. So, how do we actually do it? What does it look like to be a disciple of Jesus Christ? The beginning point is exploring what it means to be a disciple of Jesus Christ and how we grow in our relationship with him.

Week 1: Day 1
What Is a Disciple's Path?

Scripture Reading
Read the following:
  Luke 10:25-28
  Mark 12:28-34
  1 Corinthians 13:8-13
  John 13:34-35

Today's Message
A definition of discipleship based on the Gospels begins with love—love for God and love for others. *A Disciple's Path* defines a disciple in the following way:

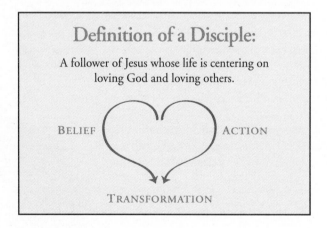

Definition of a Disciple:

A follower of Jesus whose life is centering on loving God and loving others.

BELIEF   ACTION

TRANSFORMATION

This definition of discipleship combines belief and action that result in a life transformed into the likeness of Christ.

Belief indicates that we are attracted to Jesus and his teachings. It affirms that we believe what the Gospel writers and Christian tradition say about who Jesus is. It means we trust that through the life, death, and resurrection of Jesus, God has restored our relationship with God and is at work to heal all of creation.

A disciple is an apprentice who is constantly growing in his or her understanding of what Christians believe.

But is belief enough to be considered a "follower of Jesus"? If a person has the "right" beliefs about Christ, is that sufficient? The word *follow* describes something that is done with your feet, not just with your head. Action also is required in order to be a follower of Jesus. What kind of action are we talking about? Based on today's Scripture, this action can be described as loving God and loving others. Being a disciple means we tangibly act on our deepening belief. You can be certain that you are on the path of discipleship as you act out love for God and love for others.

There are two components to following Jesus: a growth in belief and a growth in action. As the drawing illustrates, a transformed heart emerges as belief and action deepen.

Belief and action do not always grow or change at the same time or rate. For some of us, belief is enough to change action. We believe in God's redeeming love through the passion, death, and resurrection of Jesus, and as a result, we act. Many are drawn toward Christ through action as they serve others in ministries of mercy and justice, even though they are unsure about what they believe about Jesus or the church. For them, belief follows action.

Growth in belief and action marks the path along which we continue to grow as disciples of Jesus Christ. Through the combination of belief and action, transformation takes place as we become people whose lives are centering on loving God and loving others.

> "The love which our Lord requires in all his followers, is the love of God and man;—of God, for his own, and of man, for God's sake."
>
> —John Wesley[2]

The discipleship pathway is the way that we grow as followers of Christ. Following Christ is not just subscribing to and claiming a set of beliefs, rituals, or spiritual disciplines. It is a way of life.

Your Reflections

In your own words, how would you define a disciple of Jesus?

What are the beliefs that you would name as essential for a disciple of Jesus?

How have your beliefs been demonstrated by your actions?

How have your beliefs and actions changed over time?

Prayer

Lord, I want to follow you. I trust you to be at work in my life as I enter into the practices by which my life can be centered in loving you and loving others. Do your work of grace in me. Amen.

WEEK 1: DAY 2
RELATIONSHIP STAGES

Scripture Reading

Read the following:
   John 1:43-51
   Psalm 119:1-5, 57-60, 105
   Philippians 3:8-16

Today's Message

The discipleship path starts at birth and ends at death. God's grace is drawing us into relationship every moment of our existence. Our opportunity is to respond to God's invitation and enter into a growing relationship with our Creator. Day 1's reading defined a *disciple* as "a follower of Jesus whose life is centering on loving God and loving others" and suggested that following Jesus includes two essential components: growth in belief and growth in action. The discipleship pathway is the way that we deepen our relationship with Christ and the church.

Once we are grounded in the definition of a follower of Jesus, it is helpful to identify where we are in relationship with Jesus. Today you will identify where you believe you are along the relationship continuum with Jesus, which will provide a guidepost for your journey.

Relationship Stages

As we grow in relationship with Jesus, different stages might look like this:

Ignoring	Exploring	Getting Started	Going Deeper	Centering
(Strangers)	(Acquaintances)	(Friends)	(Good Friends)	(Intimate Friends)
"I don't know if I believe in God." "I believe in God, but I don't need a faith community."	"I believe in God, but I'm not sure about Jesus or the church." "My faith is not a significant part of my life."	"I believe in Jesus, and I am working on what it means to follow him." "I am participating in the life of the church."	"My relationship with Jesus makes a difference in how I live my life. I am discovering how my life can make God's love real in the world."	"Following Jesus is the most important thing in my life." "My life is part of God's transformation of the world."

Prevenient   Justifying   Sanctifying

We experience God's grace in new ways as we grow in relationship with Jesus.

Review the stages listed in the graph. Note that they are broad groupings and offer a way to look at spiritual growth. The purpose of identifying your stage is not to provide a rigid category but to give you a general idea of where you are currently in relationship with Jesus so that you can begin to identify what your next steps might be as you move more deeply into living a life that is centering on Christ.

John Wesley described the way God's grace is at work in our lives in three stages, which, in large part, mirror this growth in relationship with Jesus: **prevenient grace** (the love of God that begins to be at work in our lives long before we respond in commitment to Jesus Christ), **justifying grace** (the love of God that draws us into a new relationship with God based on God's grace in the death and resurrection of Jesus), and **sanctifying grace** (the love of God that continues to be at work in our lives to enable us to grow into a life that is fully centered in Jesus Christ). We will talk more about these stages of grace in Day 3.

Our relationship with God mirrors the way a relationship develops between two human beings. It moves from stranger, to acquaintance, to friend, to good friend, and finally to intimate friend or lover. Similarly, our relationship with God grows and moves into deeper intimacy and vulnerability as trust develops; as a result, our love for God and for our neighbor matures. As in a deepening human relationship, a key element in the development of our relationship with God is spending time together.

Prior to being introduced to someone, you likely would label the person a *stranger*. You don't know the person—who the person is and what he or she is about. The relationship is formal. There can be apprehension or fear or at least a hint of awkwardness. At this earliest stage of relationship with Jesus, these conditions can be true for those who have yet to experience the love of Christ. They don't know this stranger Jesus, nor do they know what to expect of the relationship because they haven't experienced the character of God. A person may *ignore*, be unaware of, or be disinterested in God's invitation for relationship. It simply may be that they haven't been introduced.

After interacting with a person a few times, you come to know the person, and the relationship begins to be more relaxed. Your relationship is less formal than that of a stranger, but you still are getting to know each other. You become an *acquaintance*. At this stage of faith, a person is getting to know Jesus and the church. He or she is *exploring* a relationship with Jesus. A person might state that he or she believes in God but is not sure about Jesus or the church.

The next stage in a developing relationship is *friends*. At this point you are *getting started* in a relationship. Starting a friendship means that you have decided to make a commitment to a person. You spend more time together and begin to share your life. The relationship tends to be more at ease and conversational. At this faith stage, a person might say that he or she believes in Jesus and is working on what it means to follow him. The person has made a decision to follow Jesus, has accepted God's grace, and has begun participating in the life of the church.

As the friendship develops, the next stage is *good friends*. The relationship is *going deeper*. This maturing relationship develops through increased time, commitment, and disclosure; it might be described as a relationship that makes a difference in how you live your life. At this stage of faith, a person continues to grow in belief in Jesus and in action to make God's love tangible in the world.

In the final and ongoing stage we become *intimate friends*. Increased fidelity and commitment define the relationship. In the faith relationship, it is a life that is *centering on Jesus*. Following Jesus becomes the most important thing. It's what the Apostle Paul meant when he said that nothing mattered more in his life than knowing Christ. Notice that the word is *centering* and not *centered*. It is not a fixed point but one that continues to evolve. Discipleship is a lifelong experience of continuing transformation by the grace of God.

The hope is that God will draw you into a life that is centering on Christ—one where you are in intimate relationship with God. While progressing in relationship with God moves you along the continuum, it is important to remember that the faith journey is filled with twists and turns along the way. But it is a continuing journey with God.

Your Reflections

At this time in your walk with God, how would you characterize your relationship with Jesus? Circle one:

stranger   **acquaintance**   **friend**   **good friend**   **intimate friend**

How would you describe your relationship with God?

How would you describe your relationship with the church?

How were you introduced to Jesus?

How were you introduced to the church?

How has your relationship with God changed over time?

While we walk
  with God in light,
God our hearts doth
  still unite;
Dearest fellowship
  we prove,
Fellowship in Jesus'
  love.

Sweetly each, with
  each combined,
In the bonds of duty
  joined,
Feels the cleansing
  blood applied,
Daily feels that Christ
  hath died.

Still, O Lord, our faith
  increase,
Cleanse from all
  unrighteousness,
Thee the unholy
  cannot see;
Make, O make us
  meet for Thee!
    —Charles Wesley[4]

Prayer

Lord, thank you for your love and
the way you invite me into deeper
relationship. Show me the way to grow,
and help me to center my life on you.
Amen.

Week 1: Day 3
God's Role in Growing Your Faith

Scripture Reading
Read the following:
   Ephesians 1:15-23
   Ephesians 3:14-20
   Romans 5:1-11

Today's Message
On Day 2 you identified where you are in relationship to Christ, a marker that provides a guidepost for your journey. As disciples of Jesus, we are striving to live a life that more and more centers on Christ. The good news is that it is not up to us to do this alone! God, the church, family, and each individual all have roles to play, and all of these roles interact and work together to help us grow.

All three cogs of the wheel are required. God does God's part, but we have a responsibility to respond and to put our faith into practice; and the church and family have a responsibility to provide experiences and opportunities to engage with and to nurture us as we grow. Today we will look at the role of God, who is the initiator of our faith.

God's Role: Grace in the Wesleyan Tradition
In *The Great God Brown,* famed playwright Eugene O'Neill wrote, "Man is born broken. He lives by mending. The grace of God is glue."[5] That is a fairly accurate assessment of the human condition and the means by which we humans are brought back to our originally created purpose. That is the role of God—bringing us back to our created purpose through grace. In the Methodist tradition, the "way of grace" or the "way of salvation" is more of a process than an event.

To put it simply, God's role is to mend us through God's grace. John Wesley believed that God's grace is a movement, and he described this movement as a lifelong journey that begins at the moment of birth. He described it as three progressive stages of grace: prevenient grace, justifying grace, and sanctifying grace. Notice that these three stages of grace correspond to the relationship stages we reviewed in Day 2.

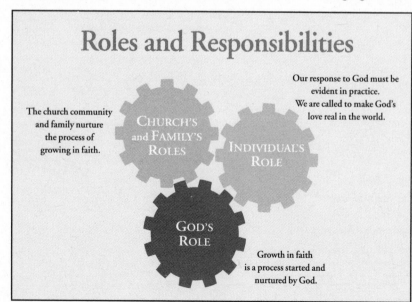

Roles and Responsibilities

CHURCH'S and FAMILY'S ROLES

INDIVIDUAL'S ROLE

GOD'S ROLE

The church community and family nurture the process of growing in faith.

Our response to God must be evident in practice. We are called to make God's love real in the world.

Growth in faith is a process started and nurtured by God.

God's Role
The Way of Grace

Prevenient Grace	Justifying Grace	Sanctifying Grace
God's grace is at work in all persons who then, through God's grace, have a choice about their response.	We are forgiven, redeemed, and called to new life through the atoning work of Jesus Christ on the cross.	We continue to grow in the likeness and image of Christ through the perfecting work of the Holy Spirit.

Wesley effectively depicted these stages of grace in his famous "house metaphor."[6]

Prevenient grace is the front porch—the initial entryway into a life of grace. Prevenient grace means that God meets us where we are, before we have made any decision to follow God. It exists prior to and without reference to anything we may have done. God is calling all persons into relationship, and we can choose how we will respond. Some of us will ignore this call. From that point, God's prevenient grace operates in a person's life to woo and lure him or her in subtle, subversive ways, giving the person the power to choose salvation and overcome his or her originally sinful state. God's grace operates prior to our recognizing or acknowledging it, and it is the very reason that we are able to baptize children.

Justifying grace is the doorway of the house. God's justifying grace declares us saved, restores us to right relationship with God, and enables us to begin the lifelong work of restoring the tarnished image of God within us. When we choose to become disciples of Christ, we are *justified* by grace. Justifying grace is offered by God to all people. We receive grace by faith and trust in Christ, through which God pardons us of sin. "For by grace you have been saved through faith, and this is not your own doing; it is the gift of God—not the result of works, so that no one may boast" (Ephesians 2:8-9). This justifying grace cancels our guilt and empowers us to resist the power of sin and to fully love God and our neighbors.

Justifying grace can occur in different ways for different people. It may happen in one transforming moment, as in response to an altar call, or it may involve a series of decisions across time. When we are justified, we leave the front porch and enter through the doorway of faith. But we are never finished. Justifying grace is the starting line.

Sanctifying grace is the inside of the house. We enter the house of sanctifying grace, which empowers us for holy living. We begin the lifelong work of restoring the full reflection of God's image within us and make the daily choices to "do no harm, do good, and stay in love with God" (Wesley's three simple rules).[7] Sanctifying grace is God's grace at work in the life of a Christian to shape his or her life into the likeness of Christ. We continue to work out our salvation as we grow in faith. Sanctifying grace is where we figure out that it is not "all about me" and begin to participate in God's redemption of the world. It is the grace of God that sustains followers in the journey toward perfection of love. This perfection is a genuine love of God with heart, soul, mind, and strength, as well as a genuine love of our neighbors as ourselves. In other words, God will perfect our love for God and our love for others.

God will initiate, nurture, and grow your faith process. So don't worry; God is leading.

Your Reflections

As you look back on your life, can you identify the times or instances in which God was wooing you or drawing you closer?

Describe how you have seen God initiate, nurture, and grow your faith.

If you can point to the time that you entered the doorway of faith, write about it here:

Hence may all our actions flow,
Love the proof that Christ we know;
Mutual love the token be,
Lord, that we belong to Thee

Love, Thine image, love impart!
Stamp it on our face and heart!
Only love to us be given!
Lord, we ask no other heaven.
—Charles Wesley[8]

Prayer

God, thank you for amazing grace. Perfect me in love, and help me to love you and others more deeply. Amen.

WEEK 1: DAY 4
THE ROLES OF THE CHURCH AND FAMILY IN GROWING YOUR FAITH

Scripture Reading

Read the following:
  1 Timothy 4:8-16
  2 Timothy 1:1-7
  Hebrews 10:19-25

Today's Message

On Day 3 you discovered the way in which God develops faith through prevenient, justifying, and sanctifying grace. Another critical component of a developing faith are the roles of the church and family. We read in Hebrews 10:25 (NIV), "Let us not give up meeting together, as some are in the habit of doing, but let us encourage one another—and all the more as you see the Day approaching." It seems that even in the early church, people had a habit of not gathering in community! Faith journeying must be done in Christian community.

The church's role is to nurture, encourage, and challenge us as we strive to grow in our love for God and others. How does God do this through the church? The church provides opportunities to experience God through small groups, corporate worship, and experiences that allow us to use our spiritual gifts in service. These three community spiritual practices nurture our faith. We put our faith into action by taking advantage of the opportunities given to us by the church. We attend worship, engage in a small group, and discover our role to serve.

Parents and primary caregivers are the principal vehicles for infusing faith in children and youth, and they determine the ways in which children will engage in worship, small groups, and service. At best, the church may have one to four hours a week to support and teach children and youth. Consider the words of Deuteronomy 6:6-7 (NIV): "These commandments that I give you today are to be upon your hearts. Impress on your children. Talk about them when you sit at home and when you walk along the road, when you lie down and when you get up." The family cannot leave to the church the teaching of faith to children. Children and youth must see faith lived at home if they are to become lifelong followers of Jesus.

Church's and Family's Roles
Opportunities to Experience God in Christian Community

Small-group Community	Corporate Worship	Gifts-based Service
Gather with other Christians in a small group to pray, learn, and grow together.	Celebrate God's presence in worship with a faith community.	Discover your spiritual gifts and participate in God's work through the ministry of the church.

O Lord, may church and home combine to teach thy perfect way, with gentleness and love like thine, that none shall ever stray.
—Carlton C. Buck[9]

Your Reflections

Describe the way in which your family influenced your faith.

If your family did not influence your faith, identify the people who did.

How were you taught faith at home?

If you were not taught faith at home, how did you learn?

How do you intend to teach faith to your children or family members who are young?

Prayer

God, thank you for the church and the people who have shown me your love.
Amen.

Week 1: Day 5
Your Role in Growing Your Faith

Scripture Reading

Read the following:
1 Corinthians 9:24-25
Romans 12:1-21

Today's Message

Over the last few days, you have reviewed several of the roles in a growing faith: God's role, and the church's and family's roles. Today we investigate the individual's role in response to God's grace.

In his first letter to the Corinthians, the Apostle Paul compares the discipleship path to an athlete training for a competitive race. He says that everyone who competes in an athletic event goes into training in order to win a crown that will not last, but we go into spiritual training to win a crown that will last forever (1 Corinthians 9:25).

Throughout Christian history, followers of Christ have engaged in certain spiritual disciplines that allow God to shape and mold us in God's image. Could Paul have been referring to spiritual disciplines? It is no different today. As we practice spiritual disciplines, God deepens our love for God and our love for our neighbor; and we become deeply committed followers of Christ.

As Christians living in the Methodist tradition, there are basic expectations of each member of the church. When we join The United Methodist Church and take membership vows, we profess faith in Jesus Christ, affirm membership in the church universal, assert loyalty to The United Methodist Church, and vow to support our local congregation through our prayers, our presence, our gifts, our service, and our witness.[10] These vows taken in worship contain the seven essential practices of discipleship which are the means by which we journey along the discipleship pathway: prayer, Scripture meditation, corporate worship, small-group community, financial generosity, gifts-based service, and invitational evangelism. We all begin at different places and do not have to be experts in any of the spiritual practices, but as we continue to move deeper in each practice, we cultivate a deeper relationship with God.

Each practice listed on the chart to the left is an expression of loving God and loving others. It is through these practices that God

---

Individual's Role

Personal Spiritual Disciplines

Prayer	Scripture Meditation	Financial Generosity	Invitational Evangelism
Practicing the spiritual discipline by spending time each day with God.	Studying and reflecting on the Bible to experience the living Word of hope in the written word of Scripture.	Practicing Christian stewardship through the biblical discipline of tithing.	Inviting others to experience God's love and become disciples of Jesus Christ.

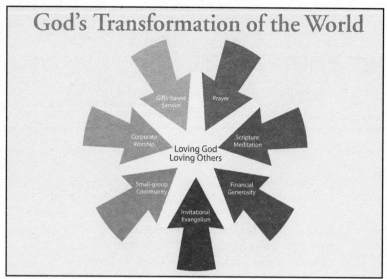

God's Transformation of the World

changes us; and as we change, the ways in which we practice these disciplines should also change.

Notice in the illustration above that as we follow Jesus through the practicing of spiritual disciplines—both individual practices (the darker arrows on the right) and corporate practices (the lighter arrows on the left)—God transforms our hearts.

Transformed hearts will always result in lives that are focused outwardly and are actively involved in making the love of God a transforming reality in the world (see the arrows pointing out in the illustration on the right). This always becomes bigger than just you or what you could do on your own. Spiritual growth impacts the whole church, community, and world. This happens individually and communally. When the whole community is growing together, amazing things happen. As we all grow together, lives are transformed, Christian community is created, and we participate in God's transformation of the world. This is all part of God's plan of salvation, and each one of us has an important role to play.

- As we practice these disciplines as individuals and as a faith community, the Holy Spirit transforms lives, creates Christian community, and heals the city and the world.
- This is God's plan for the church, and God needs us to be the community to fulfill this plan. God's plan for our lives is better than our own.

- If we do not engage, there is much transformation, community building, and healing that is left undone. As a result, lives, communities, and the world—both now and forever—are not as they could be.

Spiritual practices look different as you grow. The chart on the opposite page gives you an idea of how these practices should change. Growth in one discipline does not necessarily correspond with growth in other areas. You can explore one practice while going deeper in another. Of course, growth in these practices does not necessarily correspond with growth in what you believe. Sometimes you may change your belief, and one of these practices will change as a result. Other times, you begin with changing your actions, and through the practice of these spiritual disciplines, your beliefs are changed.

Again, growth is never as linear as the chart would lead us to believe. The discipleship pathway is seldom in a straight line, and there are always times of regression; but it is a path nevertheless, and the important thing is to keep following Jesus down the path. Wherever you are right now is all right, but it is not where you are supposed to stay indefinitely. God is never finished with us until God's work is complete in us in heaven.

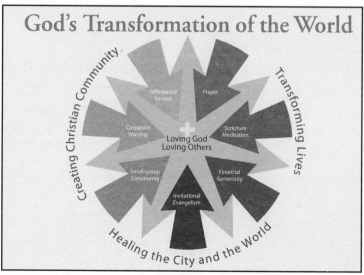

God's Transformation of the World

Spiritual Practices Change as We Grow

	Exploring	Getting Started	Going Deeper	Centering
PERSONAL SPIRITUAL DISCIPLINES – to do on my own				
PRAYER and	Formal prayers Grace before meals Lord's Prayer	Informal prayers Develop regular time/place Pray with a small group	Conversational prayer Learn different types of prayer	Contemplative prayer Silent prayer Fasting
SCRIPTURE MEDITATION	Bible reading for knowledge and understanding	Following daily Bible readings Read Bible for comfort and inspiration	Bible reading and reflection for transformation	Bible reading (daily) Bible reflection (daily) Lectio Divina
FINANCIAL GENEROSITY	Occasional giving	Regular giving	Tithing	Sacrificial generosity beyond the tithe
INVITATIONAL EVANGELISM	Explore questions about Jesus Christ	Get to know the gospel story and your story	Find opportunities to share your witness	Help others share their witness
CHRISTIAN COMMUNITY – to do with others				
SMALL-GROUP COMMUNITY	Newcomer class Low-commitment group Exploring faith class	Short-term class Bible study group Sunday school	Relationship-focused group (for accountability, fellowship, Bible study, service, and prayer) Long-term Bible study	Guided by spiritual mentor Lead others in small-group, covenant group Discipleship accountability group
CORPORATE WORSHIP	Occasional participation in worship and Communion	Familiarity with elements of corporate worship and Communion	Transformative participation in worship and Communion	Experience the significance and power of corporate worship and Communion
GIFTS-BASED SERVICE	Serve where needed	Discover your spiritual gifts and serve out of giftedness	Discern God's call	Live out God's call and equip others to serve

Your Reflections

Review the spiritual practices chart.

Of the seven spiritual practices, which ones are most comfortable for you?

With which practice do you have the least experience?

On the chart above, circle where you think you are in each of the practices.
For example, beside financial generosity, circle one of the following: occasional giving, regular giving, tithing, or sacrificial generosity beyond the tithe.

> "O begin! Fix some part of every day for private exercises. You may acquire the taste which you have not: What is tedious at first, will afterwards be pleasant. Whether you like it or no, read and pray daily. It is for your life; there is no other way; else you will be a trifler all your days."
> —John Wesley[11]

Reflect on your current practice of the spiritual disciplines and how you would like to grow in each of the practices. Record your thoughts below:

To go deeper in your experience of God's grace and love, see *A Disciple's Heart: Growing in Love and Grace* (Abingdon Press, 2015).

Prayer

God, thank you for the church, the people who have shown me your love. Help me to engage in the spiritual practices that will grow me in Jesus' likeness and image. Amen.

WEEK 2: PRAYERS
PRAYER AND SCRIPTURE MEDITATION

It has been said that the local church is sometimes like a football game. There are fifty thousand people in the stands in need of exercise and twenty-two people on the field in need of rest. Unfortunately, for many people Christianity is a spectator sport. They expect church leaders to do the ministry, and they just want to be fed and nourished. That understanding of the church is quite foreign in the New Testament, where we find numerous instances of growing, involved, passionate Christians intentionally working out their faith in tangible acts of prayer, offering, and service.

One term used to describe this kind of ordered, deliberate practice of the faith is *spiritual discipline*. Spiritual disciplines are the daily habits or practices of the Christian walk that prepare us for life's toughest challenges, free us to experience the love and grace of God in community, and prepare us to face death. They are the practical tools by which we follow the path that leads to a life that is centering on loving God and loving others.

When we become members of The United Methodist Church, we promise to support the ministries of the church by our "prayers, presence, gifts, service, and witness."[1] This week we will look at the first practice, prayer. Specifically, we will focus on the spiritual disciplines of daily prayer rooted in reflection on Scripture. Prayer and Scripture meditation are the primary ways we communicate with God.

To engage with the game of life, we need a coach—someone to teach, support, and encourage us. As Christians, the Holy Spirit is our Coach, our Supporter, and our Encourager. Just as athletes who regularly study off the field and allow their coach to mentor them are the most successful and faithful players, so it is with us in our faith walk. As we grow in belief and action, we spend more time with our Coach, studying the Scriptures and connecting through prayer.

Are you a spectator Christian? Are you willing to jump onto the field and play? Are you ready to get into the game?

WEEK 2: DAY 1
WHAT IS PRAYER?

Scripture Reading

Read the following, noticing how the Lord's Prayer differs in these Gospels:

Luke 11:1-4
Matthew 6:9-14

Today's Message

What is prayer? How would you define it? The primary purpose of prayer is to develop an intimate relationship with God. Prayer is simply talking and listening to God. It is a time to open ourselves to God—a time to talk with God and share our joys, fears, and challenges. It also is a time to listen. As in any human relationship, we must create time for God in order for our relationship with God to deepen.

If you are or ever have been in a committed relationship, think about what would happen if you rarely talked or spent time with your partner. What if you only spent one hour a week in conversation with him or her? What would that relationship look like?

Building intimacy in a human relationship requires careful attention and intentional discipline. In the same way, prayer is about cultivating a relationship with God, and that also takes time. During Jesus' brief ministry, often he went off by himself to pray. When the disciples observed his practice of prayer and asked him to teach them to pray, he gave them—and us—a wonderful model of prayer. We call it the Lord's Prayer. It provides a practical pattern of prayer for us to follow—adoration, surrender, supplication (asking), confession, and commitment.

Read the prayer in the left column very slowly. Remember there is a vast difference between speaking a prayer and praying!

Father, hallowed be your name.	*Adoration*
Your kingdom come.	*Surrender*
Give us each day our daily bread.	*Supplication*
And forgive us our sins,	*Confession*
for we ourselves forgive everyone indebted to us.	*Commitment to Follow*
And do not bring us to the time of trial.	*Supplication[2]*

Whether you have a little or a lot of experience with prayer, it is our hope that *A Disciple's Path* will help you develop and deepen your prayer life.

Your Reflections

How do you pray?

How often?

Where do you pray? Describe your favorite prayer place.

Do you carve intentional time out of your day to talk with God? If yes, when?

> "You may as well expect a child to grow without food as a soul without private prayer."
>
> —John Wesley[3]

If no, what would be the best time of the day for you to consistently talk and listen to God?

How do you listen to God?

Prayer

Pray the Lord's Prayer several times. Say it very slowly, reflecting on the different phrases of the prayer.

WEEK 2: DAY 2
THREE PRAYER METHODS

Scripture Reading
Read the following:
    Philippians 4:4-7
    Psalm 139:1-14, 23-24
    Luke 18:9-14

Today's Message
One of the twenty-two questions John Wesley gave to members of his discipleship groups was this: "Am I enjoying prayer?"[4] He thought it was a very important question.

Are you enjoying prayer? Prayer is as easy as a conversation. Sometimes it helps to use written prayers, but there is a point at which prayer is just like talking and listening to a close friend, spouse, or partner. It is sharing your heart and soul with God, who desires to have a close and intimate relationship with you. There are so many ways to pray that we couldn't possibly cover them all in this workbook. But at their core, all forms of prayer work as a method to increase our conscious contact with God in everyday life and to connect us to Jesus Christ, our King, Prophet, and Redeemer.

Today we will look at three forms of prayer: 1) ACTS, 2) five finger prayer, and 3) the Jesus Prayer.

ACTS: ACTS is an acronym for Adoration, Confession, Thanksgiving, and Supplication. Those elements, as you saw in Day 1, are modeled for us in the Lord's Prayer. You can personalize them as they relate to your life.

Examples:
Lord, your amazing love and power continue to astound me! Your presence in my life continues to be my rock. (Adoration)

I have been complaining and upset most of the day, and I confess my ingratitude for my job, my family, and my health. I have been judging people at work and am angry with my boss. Lord, help me to be grateful and to respond to others as you would have me to do. (Confession)

Thank you, God, for the blessings in my life. I am grateful for my health, my resources, and even my challenges that seem to provide me the opportunity to rely on you more and deepen our relationship. (Thanksgiving)

Lord, I ask that you will be with my grandmother who is dying and that she might feel your presence in her time of transition. Please guide me in work and family decisions. I pray for the knowledge of your will and the power to carry it out. (Supplication)

Note that ACTS does not include listening. You might set aside time to hear God through silence, journaling, or solitude, or to experience other methods of prayer that cultivate silence and solitude.

Write out your ACTS prayer below as it relates to your life today:

A (adoration)

C (confession)

T (thanksgiving)

S (supplication)

Five finger prayer: This is a simple prayer that you can remember by looking at your hand. Each finger represents a group of people:

- The thumb, which is closest to you, represents those who are nearest to you. These are your family and loved ones. Pray daily that God will guide and direct them.
- The pointer finger represents those who point you to God. They might include your pastor, prayer partners, members of your small group, church leaders, spiritual mentors, and so forth.
- The middle finger, which is the longest finger, represents leaders in the church and world, including government and business leaders. These people shape our lives and our world, and they need God's guidance.

- The fourth finger, the ring finger, is the weakest. This finger represents those who are weak and in need. They might be poor or marginalized, or they might be in trouble and pain. Whatever the need might be, they are in desperate need of your prayers.
- The little finger is the smallest finger, and it represents you. After you have prayed for the other four groups, you can spend time praying for your needs. This finger will remind you to keep your needs in proper perspective, which will help you pray for yourself more effectively.

For families: Try doing this five finger prayer with your children. If you want, write out the prayer ahead of time.

Contemplative prayer: There are many ways to increase your awareness of God's presence. Contemplative prayer is a way of making yourself aware of the constant presence of God. There are a variety of ways to move into contemplative prayer, including centering prayer, *Lectio Divina*, praying the Psalms, labyrinths, and many others. Followers of Christ in the early church used the Jesus Prayer, found in Luke 18:13, to increase their awareness of God's presence and as a way to commune with God. A common form of the Jesus Prayer is this: "Lord Jesus Christ, have mercy on me, a sinner." It also can be shortened to "Lord, have mercy" or "Jesus, have mercy."

Spend some time praying the Jesus Prayer. Repeat the Jesus Prayer gently, allowing the words to focus your attention on God while simultaneously expressing your need for grace. Try it for three to five minutes. When you notice your mind wandering, return to the prayer.

Your Reflections

Reflect and write about your experience with the Jesus Prayer. What was it like to be in silence?

How often do you practice silence and solitude? What do you like or dislike about it?

How often do you set aside intentional time to connect with God in prayer?

Describe how and when you pray:

Prior to today, had you ever practiced the ACTS (adoration, confession, thanksgiving, supplication) method of prayer? If so, what has been your experience with this prayer method?

Do you have experience in practicing contemplative prayer? If so, describe it.

Would you say that you are comfortable with prayer? Why or why not?

What are your greatest difficulties with prayer?

What could be your next step toward growth in the practice of payer?

> "Prayer is not primarily saying words or thinking thoughts. It is, rather, a stance. It's a way of living in the Presence. It is, further, a way of living in awareness of the Presence, even enjoying the Presence. The full contemplative is not just aware of the Presence, but trusts, allows, and delights in it."
>
> —Richard Rohr[5]

Prayer
Lord, teach me how to pray and increase
my awareness of your presence in my life.
Amen.

Week 2: Day 3
The Bible

Scripture Reading

Read the following:
Psalm 119:97-105, 129-133
2 Timothy 3:10-17

Today's Message

A Disciple's Path includes and encourages regular study of the Scriptures in community and in solitude. John Wesley referred to himself as a "man of one book" *(homo unius libri)* and challenged his followers to follow his example.[6] As you engage with the Bible, you can trust the Holy Spirit to make the written word a living word in your experience.

The Bible is a book for the community of faith first—not just the individual. It instructs us how to do life together and what our roles and responsibilities are as members of the community of God. It is a book of books about God and God's people. It is what we have experienced of God over many centuries—what we have recorded about God's activities and interactions with Israel and the ancient world. God longs to be known, and the Bible is one of the means by which God is revealed to us. As United Methodists, we believe that the Bible is the inspired record of the people who experienced the active Word of God. In this sense, *inspired* does not mean that God dictated text to passive note takers; it means that God's presence was breathed into it and God's truth is at the central core.

What follows in the remainder of "Today's Message" are helpful tips for reading and studying the Bible from Diana Hynson's article "De-Mystifying the Bible (at Least a Little Bit),"
which appeared on the General Board of Discipleship website.[7] Some additional thoughts have been added to the material, and these appear in italics.

First, and most important—don't be afraid to read it and try to figure it out on your own. . . . The Bible is a book of books, written over time. *There are many understandings of who wrote the Bible, and there are numerous contributors.* Suffice it to say that much of the Old Testament, at least, was shared as oral history before being written and collected.

The Bible books are not in chronological or historical order (which is sometimes highly inconvenient!). *Everything in the Old Testament happened before the New Testament, and the first five books of the Old Testament are roughly in some chronological order, but not the Prophets, for example. All of the Gospels were written after the letters of Paul, and Paul's letters are in order of length, not date.* What this means is that you need to do a bit of historical homework by reading the introduction to the biblical book in a good study Bible to help get oriented to the time, cultural location, and so on.

The chapter and line verses were not original to the texts, but added to aid in our reading and organization.

Some books have the same name. That 1, 2, or 3 before the name of a book means something. There are two letters to the Corinthians, for example, and they are not the same.

There are a multitude of translations and paraphrases of the Bible, and they are not all equally good. Translations try to use the original language and translate the original word into our language.

Paraphrases do not try to translate word for word, but thought to thought. You might want to have more than one "flavor" to help with understanding. The New Revised Standard Version *and the* New International Version *are the two biblical translations used in the highly acclaimed* The New Interpreter's Bible *commentary series. Those Bibles were translated from the original texts of the ancient Scriptures from (mainly) Hebrew and Greek.*

The Bible means what it means, but not necessarily just exactly what it says. Virtually any specific text is interpreted somehow. *While this statement can open a huge debate on the doctrine of Scripture and the interpretation of Scripture, we can probably agree that Scripture should be studied. When it says something happened in forty days or forty years, for example, that may really mean a generation or a general passage of time.*

There are some teachings, laws, practices, and portrayals of God that seem troubling and difficult to believe. Some are more benign, like the law against eating pork (Leviticus 11:3-8) or shellfish (11:9-12) . . . and Christians typically ignore them. Others are much more difficult. Some seem excessively bloodthirsty (1 Samuel 15:1-3 or Psalm 137:7-9, for example) or contradictory (see for example Matthew 10:34 and John 16:32-33). How do we reconcile all this?

- First, return to the issues of culture and history.
- Second, depend on the wisdom of the community.

- Third, weigh the text against your best biblical/theological understanding of love, grace, accountability, and justice. *This may be another way to ask, "What would Jesus do or understand?"*

As United Methodists, we consider another set of interpretive tools, which we refer to as the Wesleyan Quadrilateral: Scripture, interpreted through tradition, reason, and experience. We will look at the Wesleyan Quadrilateral on Day 4.

So, in short form, keep these questions in mind:

- What do I think this Scripture passage means?
- What do I know of the history, culture, and context of this passage and time period? How is God/Jesus/the Holy Spirit presented in this passage, and is it consistent with the broad range of what we know and have experienced?
- How does it square with a biblical/theological understanding of love, grace, accountability, and justice?
- What might God be saying to the community and also to me through the Bible?
- How does the community confirm (or not) what I think is true about it?

Your Reflections

Do you own a Bible? If yes, when did you receive it, and what translation is it? (If you need assistance in selecting a Bible, see pages 112-15 in the Appendix and talk with your small-group leader.)

Before taking this class, when was the last time you read the Bible?

When was the last time you studied and reflected on the Bible?

Do you feel comfortable reading the Bible? If not, why?

What translations of the Bible do you own? Write them below, and circle the one you prefer to use.

> "[The Bible] is more than a record. . . . It is the proclamation which brings about what it proclaims. It not only offers liberty, it sets [us] free. It does more than promise sight; it 'opens blind eyes.'"
> —Paul Scherer[8]

Prayer

Dear God, thank you for sharing your story with us. Please help me to study and reflect on your word on my own and with others. Amen.

WEEK 2: DAY 4
THE WESLEYAN QUADRILATERAL

Scripture Reading

Read the following:

Matthew 7:24-27

2 Timothy 1:8-14

Today's Message

The Bible doesn't provide a specific answer to critical issues such as nuclear proliferation or genetic cloning. As individuals, we wrestle with complex questions that cannot be answered by quoting a specific verse of Scripture. As a result, thoughtful Christians need a way to reflect on Scripture and discern God's will. John Wesley offered three tools to use when interpreting Scripture and applying it to our lives. They are church tradition, reason, and experience.

United Methodists label Wesley's approach as the Wesleyan Quadrilateral, a term that was coined by Albert Outler in the 1960s while serving on the commission on doctrine and doctrinal standards for The United Methodist Church.[9] It has become the framework within which we are called to apply the truth of Scripture to our personal and social lives.

Scripture: The Bible is the primary authority for our faith. We study the Scriptures prayerfully, looking for connections to the life we live and the decisions we are called to make. The Bible is our map, our guide, and our GPS system. It speaks to us about what God expects of our lives, our thoughts, and our actions. Though written long ago in different cultures, it is very pertinent and relevant today.

Tradition: We interpret Scripture with guidance from the teaching, belief, and practice of fellow Christians across two millennia of church history. The writings on theology, doctrine, and the texts of councils and of saints can guide us in judgment. More specifically, we listen to Scripture through our own tradition through the Anglican branch of the Protestant Reformation. As United Methodists, we also look to the *Discipline* and *The Book of Resolutions of The United Methodist Church,* which express the wisdom of the representative bodies of our denomination.

Reason: Wesley knew that God gave us brains and expects us to use them as we wrestle with the truth of Scripture. Reason alone can be dangerous in that it can be manipulated and lead us astray; but combined with tradition and experience, it becomes the means by which we sort out the application of Scripture to our life situations. At our church we like to say, "When you come to church, you don't have to shift your mind into neutral when you put your car in park!"

Experience: The *Discipline* describes experience as "the personal appropriation of God's forgiving and empowering grace."[11] It is the often diverse way in which our personal and community life informs the way Scripture speaks to us. It is the way in which the written word becomes a living Word in our lives.

> "Wesley believed that the living core of the Christian faith was revealed in Scripture, illumined by tradition, vivified in personal experience, and confirmed by reason."
> —The *Discipline*[10]

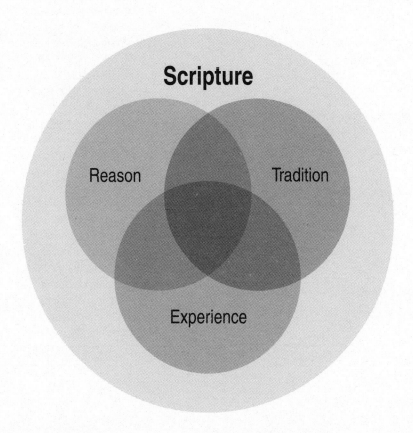

Scripture

Reason

Tradition

Experience

United Methodists believe that all four components of the Quadrilateral are important in order to prevent us from being anchored in the way things always have been or making religion an entirely subjective, personal exercise. The Quadrilateral is a system of balance and equilibrium—a hallmark of Wesleyan thought.

Your Reflections

How do you begin to develop your convictions on moral, ethical, or personal concerns?

Typically we develop our convictions through our personal experience, the beliefs of others we respect, and what we read and hear through the media. Think of one of the most hotly contested issues of the day as it relates to Christianity. Write below how you feel about it and why:

How have tradition, reason, and experience influenced your understanding of Scripture?

Describe a time when you used Scripture to inform your decisions.

"Wesley knew that the transformed life was not accidental. He was convinced that one does not drift into inward or outward holiness. God's grace required response and that response included a careful reading, reflection upon, and incorporation of and obedience to scripture in everyday living. God's grace was always available and scripture was one way for Christians to appropriate that grace into daily life."
—Rueben Job[12]

Prayer

Dear God, thank you for the gift of your Son, Jesus Christ. Thank you, Lord, for the God-given resources of the Holy Scriptures, church tradition, reason, and experience. May they shape us in your likeness and image. Amen.

WEEK 2: DAY 5
BIBLE STUDY AND REFLECTION

Scripture Reading

Read the following:
    Psalm 119:9-18

Today's Message

A Disciple's Path focuses on practices of discipleship that shape people in the love of God revealed in Jesus Christ. Prayer and Scripture meditation are the two spiritual practices we are focusing on this week.

Let's be clear: the Bible does no good if you don't pick it up. The less time you spend in prayer, the more likely your relationship with Christ will stagnate—or, even worse, backslide. We live in a busy world, one that tells us that slowing down to spend time with God is unnecessary or impractical. Self-reliance is a huge value in our culture, yet in many ways it is in direct opposition to the gospel. We must rely on God and have the willingness and capability to be God reliant. We have to build trust with God, and that takes time, intentionality, and work—just as in human relationships. And just as the human relationships you devote your attention to benefit, so great fruit will come as a result of your intentionality in your relationship with God.

The Bible is not a textbook. Nor is it a manual to be studied, mastered, and mechanically applied. Most of the Bible was written in common language and given orally to illiterate people. It is important to understand the *context* of the Bible, knowing the parts that are oral tradition, poetry, and letters written to faith communities. It also is helpful to know the audience, culture, and context of the time period. It is best to study these things in community because a deeper meaning and experience can come from a group. Eventually, though, it is very important to humbly "listen" to the Scriptures so that they can read us rather than us reading them. In other words, we must allow the text to penetrate us as a painting, a poem, or a song penetrates the receiver.

Today you will explore two ways to reflect on the Bible. One is called SOAPY, and the other is the ancient practice of *Lectio Divina*.

SOAPY stands for Scripture, Observation, Application, Prayer, and Yield. The following explanation and example are adapted from the journaling work of United Methodist Bishop Dick Wills and are based on the teaching of Wayne Cordeiro of New Hope Christian Fellowship in Honolulu.[13]

1. Read the passages. As you are reading, take note of anything the Lord impresses on you as a personal word to be applied. When you read with an open heart, God will give you words of encouragement, direction, and correction (2 Timothy 3:16).
2. When God has revealed a special lesson of life to you, record what God has just shown you in your journal.
3. Title the page.
4. **Scripture**: Write down the verse you have chosen as a lesson for the day.
5. **Observation**: Write down what the lesson is for you for that day.

6. Application: Write how this lesson applies to your life.
7. Prayer: Write a prayer to God concerning this lesson and your life.
8. Yield: Write what you must yield in your life for this lesson to become alive in you.
9. Allow the Scripture to guide you in spending personal time with God in prayer.

EXAMPLE:
S: Luke 11:34. Your eye is the lamp of your body. When your eye is healthy, your whole body is full of light, but when it is bad, your body is full of darkness.

O: What I read determines the kind of light or darkness which will fill my mind and my body. I become what I think.

A: This morning as I read this Scripture, I became aware once again how important this time in Scripture is for me each day. I begin my day with reading God's Word for me. This daily reading is really what changes my life to be more like Jesus and this reading shapes my heart so it will be more useable by the Lord. I know if I miss a morning because I have an early trip to make, then there is a loss in my life and I find a small amount of darkness comes into my life. I can hardly imagine how my life would have been without this daily time in the Word so my mind and body can sample the light of God and my heart can be shaped and made more useful to the Lord.

P: Father, thank you for the gift of your Word. Thank you also for the light it brings into my mind and body as you teach and encourage me each day to be a follower of Jesus.

Y: I will not skip a day of this discipline because I need this light in my heart and mind and body.

Lectio Divina is an ancient practice of prayerful meditation of Scripture in which you listen to what Christ has to say. Its purpose is for conversion, not theology. In other words, it is not studying the Bible or trying to understand the text in our heads. Theology is for the head and is very important. *Lectio Divina*, however, is primarily for the soul. It is a way to get in touch with the Spirit of God. *Lectio Divina* is possibly one of the earliest forms of prayer, and it seeks to personalize the Scripture. It is a practical way for Christ to communicate with us and cultivate our relationship with him. It comes from Latin and means "divine reading."

Lectio: Slow, meditative reading of Scripture.
Meditation: Thinking or reflecting on the word or phrase. Why did it stand out? Why did it strike your heart?
Oratio: Your response to the word. Respond to the word. Tell God how you feel.
Contemplation: Resting in God in silence—without words, thoughts, or images.

Practical Guidelines for *Lectio Divina*
Step 1
- Say a prayer, believing that God is going to speak to you and has something to say.
- Select a short passage of Scripture, no more than one to five verses. A great place to start in the Bible for *Lectio Divina* is the Psalms or the Gospels.
- Read it **aloud** very, very slowly—almost exaggeratingly. Scripture is meant to be heard with the ears and soul. This first reading will give you the context of the passage.
- Prayerfully read the same passage a second time. Let the Scripture read you, rather than you reading the Scripture.
- Upon the third reading, read very slowly until a word or phrase touches your heart. *Then stop!*

Step 2
- Say the word or phrase aloud and begin to reflect on it.
- Ask yourself, *Why did it strike my heart? How is it pertinent to my life?*
- If you have a journal, begin to write in it, recording how the word is speaking to you.

Step 3
- Respond to the word from your heart. Tell God your feelings (either by journaling or talking silently or out loud).

Step 4
- Rest in God in silence (if you are familiar with using centering prayer—see http://www.centeringprayer.com).
- As your mind begins to wander, use the word or phrase the Spirit gave you to center again.

Scripture Reading

Read Mark 12:28-34 and use the SOAPY method.

Scripture: Write the verse you have chosen as a lesson for the day.

Observation: Write what the lesson is for you today.

Application: Write how this lesson applies to your life.

Tips for Using Both SOAPY and *Lectio Divina*

Time: Selecting a time is important. Using the same time every day leads to a daily habit of prayer that becomes highly effective.

Place: Try to find a place that is free from distractions.

Preparation: Prior to reading, it is important to engage in an activity that quiets your mind and moves you toward a more peaceful state. You might take a minute or two and take deep breaths or say a prayer inviting God to guide your prayer time.

Prayer: Write a prayer to God concerning this lesson and your life.

Yield: Write what you must yield in your life for this lesson to become alive in you.

Now read John 1:1-15 and practice *Lectio Divina* following the steps outlined previously.

Record your word or phrase here:

How did God speak to you in the passage?

Your Reflections

Describe your experience using the SOAPY method of reflecting on Scripture.

Do you think SOAPY might work for you as a prayer practice?
Why or why not?

What are your thoughts after using *Lectio Divina*?

Do you think you might like to use *Lectio Divina* more often? Why or why not?

How often do you set aside intentional time to reflect on the Bible?

How *familiar* are you with the Bible?

What could be your next step toward growth in the practice of Scripture meditation?

> "It is impossible to live as a Christian if we are un-attached to God. Our spiritual and even our physical lives become a shambles without the constant companionship with God that prayer alone can make possible."
> —Rueben Job[14]

Prayer

Dear God, help me to learn what you want me to learn and hear what you want me to hear. Guide me in your light and love. Amen.

Week 3: Presence
Corporate Worship
and Small-group Community

Each of us has an instinctual desire to belong. The African word *ubuntu* captures that desire by saying that we are people through other people; we find our humanity in connection with others.[1] A self-made individual is an oxymoron. I am who I am because you are who you are.

The spirit of *ubuntu* is exhibited in the book of Acts as Luke describes the way the first followers of Christ devoted themselves to the apostles' teaching, to fellowship with one another, to the breaking of bread, and to prayer. They met in the temple courts, fellowshipped in one another's homes, and praised God as more people came to know and experience the gospel (see Acts 2:43-47). It is a pattern of Christian community for us to follow as well.

As United Methodists, we affirm our belonging to one another in the vow of "presence," which combines spiritual disciplines of *corporate worship* and *small-group community*. We gather together in worship and small-group life to experience God, praise God, know God, and grow together as disciples of Jesus Christ so that we become a part of God's transformation of the world.

This week we will explore the importance of the spiritual discipline of presence in worship and small-group life. These two community practices are primarily done in the context of the local church. These practices are essential for us as followers of Jesus trying to learn and experience what it means to be formed into his likeness.

"Everyone who belongs to Christ belongs to
   everyone who belongs to Christ.
   You do not have to seek for unity. You have it—
   in Christ."—E. Stanley Jones[2]

WEEK 3: DAY 1
THERE IS NO SOLO CHRISTIANITY

Scripture Reading
Read the following:
   John 15:1-11

> *"'Holy solitaries' is a phrase no more consistent with the gospel than holy adulterers. The gospel of Christ knows of no religion, but social; no holiness but social holiness." —John Wesley*[3]

Today's Message
   The Methodist movement was born at Oxford University with small groups of students who were searching for a deeper relationship with God and became more methodical in their practice of worship, study, fellowship, and accountability. As the movement grew, John Wesley organized his followers into three levels of organization for gatherings. They were (1) the society (Sunday worship), (2) the weekly class meeting (small-group gathering, mixed gender), and (3) the bands (more intimate gatherings for the mature in faith, same gender).

   Wesley's model demonstrates that being a follower of Jesus means being in community with other followers of Jesus. We can be religious or spiritual without the presence of other people in our lives, but we cannot be growing disciples of Jesus Christ without the encouragement, guidance, wisdom, and accountability of other disciples. Our culture, however, tells us that spirituality is an individual thing between a person and God and is not to be shared, experienced, or dialogued with others.

   In the Scriptures, the life of faith is persistently communal. Biblically speaking, *solitary salvation* is an oxymoron, a contradiction in terms. Throughout the Old Testament, living by faith means being a part of God's community of the covenant people in the lineage of Abraham and Sarah. In the New Testament, salvation—our new relationship with God—means becoming a part of the "new creation" in the body of Christ. When we are born again, we are born into a family of brothers and sisters whom we did not choose. They are given to us in the love of God. Being saved does not mean holding a solitary ticket for a solo flight to heaven; rather, it means becoming an important part in the body of Christ. In community we learn to love God and love others and learn how to participate in God's transformation of the world—both now and forever.

   At the Last Supper, Jesus described the way we are connected to him and to one another with the analogy of the vine and branches (John 15:1-11). This text is the focus of today's "Scripture Reading."

> "Without Jesus there can be no church; and without the church we cannot stay united with Jesus. I've yet to meet anyone who has come closer to Jesus by forsaking the church."
>
> —Henri Nouwen[4]

Your Reflections

Think about what happens when a branch gets cut off from the trunk. How is that similar to people being separated from the faith community?

Do you agree that in order to be a disciple, a follower of Jesus, you can't do it alone? Why or why not?

List the reasons why people attend weekly worship.

List the things (and excuses) that keep people from attending weekly worship.

List the reasons why people participate in small groups and Bible studies.

List the things (and excuses) that keep people from participating in small groups and Bible studies.

Reflect on how you will abide in God in community.

Blest be the dear uniting love
that will not let us part;
our bodies may far off remove,
we still are one in heart.

Joined in one spirit to our Head,
where he appoints we go,
and still in Jesus' footsteps tread,
and do his work below.

We all are one who him receive,
and each with each agree,
in him the One, the Truth, we live;
blest point of unity!

Partakers of the Savior's grace,
the same in mind and heart,
nor joy, nor grief, nor time, nor place,
nor life, nor death can part.
—Charles Wesley[5]

Prayer

Heavenly Father, I can't do it alone. I need fellowship and guidance from others. Connect me to you through the people you have—or plan to have—in my life. Amen.

WEEK 3: DAY 2
PREPARING FOR WORSHIP

Scripture Reading
Read the following:
  Psalm 122
  Isaiah 6:1-8

Today's Message
Have you ever been talking with someone and suddenly you realize that you haven't been "present" to a word the person has said? Let's be honest. Sometimes it's hard to be truly present. There is a difference between presence and attendance. You can be somewhere in body but disconnected from the place emotionally, spiritually, or intellectually. Our minds often drive us from the moment, diverting us from presence. For some reason it is difficult to be completely "there."

Being present for worship is being aware and plugged in to the situations and people around you. You can prepare for worship intentionally with spiritual practices. Talking to God, reading Scripture, and including God in your days during the week increase the likelihood that you will be able to be present to God's presence during worship.

When the Jewish people prepared for worship, they were passionate. Psalms 120–130 are the songs of ascent they shouted out and sang as they walked up the hill to the Jerusalem temple. They had enthusiasm and energy as they sensed a forthcoming experience of God. They expected God to be present when they worshiped. Do you?

> "Worship is the submission of all our nature to God. It is the quickening of conscience by his holiness; the nourishment of mind with his truth; the purifying of the imagination by his beauty; the opening of the heart to his love; the surrender of will to his purpose—and all of this gathered up in adoration, the most selfless emotion of which our nature is capable and therefore the chief remedy of that self-centredness which is our original sin and the source of all actual sin."
>
> —Archbishop William Temple[6]

Your Reflections

How do you prepare for worship?

What does *presence* mean to you? How do you become present in worship?

What aspects of worship are most meaningful to you?

When was the last time you went to worship with the expectation that God would touch your life?

How is entering the sanctuary different from entering a concert hall or sports arena?

What are the factors that influence your experience of worship?

What can you do to make that shift in your mind and heart?

Prayer

LORD, I have heard of your fame;
    I stand in awe of your deeds, O LORD.
Renew them in our day,
    in our time make them known;
    in wrath remember mercy.
Amen.

(Habakkuk 3:2 NIV)

WEEK 3: DAY 3
WHAT IS WORSHIP? HOW DO WE WORSHIP AS UNITED METHODISTS?

Scripture Reading

Read the following:
 Psalm 100
 Psalm 149:1-4

Today's Message

Why do Christians gather in worship? What does worship mean to you?

Today we'll take a brief look at worship, offer background regarding Christian worship, and explain the flow of a traditional United Methodist worship service. If you did not grow up in church, the word *liturgy* may be new to you. Liturgy is a prescribed ritual for public worship and is derived from the Greek *leitourgia*, which means "work of the people."[7] When we go to worship, we literally get to work with the business of being a Christian community. That is our job description for worship. Figuratively speaking, we are hired at baptism to give praise to God in the presence of God's people. The Jews gathered together on the Sabbath (Saturday) and participated in Scripture reading and responsive prayers. A series of petitions were read or sung by a leader, and responses were made by the congregation. Set times for prayer during the day also were established and followed by the Jews.

Jesus and the early disciples, including the Apostle Paul, were Jewish and worshiped as Jews. Christian worship moved to Sunday as a weekly celebration of the resurrection. The service of the Mass in the Roman Catholic Church found its roots in the early liturgy traditions of the Jews. It consisted primarily of psalms, hymns, and readings. Together with the Mass, this liturgy constituted the official public prayer life of the Roman Catholic Church until the Reformation in the sixteenth century, led by Martin Luther.

The Church of England came into being as a part of the Reformation when the pope refused to grant King Henry VIII a divorce. Although the Church of England maintained a strong preference for Roman Catholic practices in worship, Protestant forms of worship were adopted and set in place in the *Book of Common Prayer* (1662), which continues to be the basis for worship in the Anglican tradition.

The United Methodist Church traces its history to the Church of England, in which both John and Charles Wesley were ordained as priests. Methodism began in the eighteenth century as a movement for spiritual renewal within the Church of England and did not become a separate denomination until after the American Revolution. As Methodism spread across the American continent, it was influenced by the camp meeting and revival movement on the American frontier. As a result, United Methodist worship continues to carry the rich liturgical traditions of Anglican worship while incorporating the vitality and revivalistic pragmatism of the American frontier. More recently, our worship has been enriched by contributions from United Methodist congregations around the world.

Within Methodism today there are many different worship styles and orders of worship. Yet at the center of any worship style is a gathering of people who assemble in unity to worship the triune God—Father, Son, and Holy Spirit. John 4:24 says that we are to worship in spirit and truth. What is important is not the style of worship but the genuineness of our worship.

Regardless of the worship style, there are four primary elements in the order of a worship service in the Methodist tradition.

Basic Order of Worship:
1. Gathering/entrance
2. Proclamation of the word
3. Response to the word
4. Sending forth

These basic elements of worship will take on distinctive forms based on the mission, tradition, ethnic traditions, cultural setting, and community in which the church lives. You'll find more information in *The United Methodist Book of Worship* and *The United Methodist Hymnal*. This may be the opportunity for you to explore the traditions and practices that have shaped worship in your congregation.

Your Reflections

How often do you engage in corporate worship?

Describe a time when you felt deeply connected with God's people in worship.

> "There is no Liturgy in the world, either in ancient or modern language, which breathes more of a solid, scriptural, rational piety, than the Common Prayer of the Church of England."
> —John Wesley[8]

Some churches place their baptismal font in the narthex (lobby) of the worship space, which is reminiscent of the Jewish people preparing for worship through ritual cleansing prior to coming into the temple. How might you prepare yourself spiritually before entering the sanctuary in order to experience and worship God more fully?

Theologian Søren Kierkegaard once said that many churches have a model of worship in which the people leading worship are the actors, God is the off-stage director, and the congregation is the audience. He offered a better understanding by saying that the people leading worship should be the directors, the congregation should be understood to be the actors, with God as the audience. How does this analogy change your perspective on what happens—or should happen—in worship?

The next time you are in worship, reflect on the order of worship. Does there seem to be a reason that the elements are in a particular order? If not, what questions do you have about the order of worship?

Jesus, we look to Thee,
Thy promised presence claim;
Thou in the midst of us shall be,
Assembled in Thy Name.

We meet, the grace to take
Which Thou hast freely giv'n;
We meet on earth for Thy dear sake
That we may meet in Heav'n.

Present we know Thou art;
But, O, Thyself reveal!
Now, Lord, let ev'ry waiting heart
The mighty comfort feel.

—Charles Wesley[9]

What could be your next step toward growth in the practice of corporate worship?

Prayer

God, I give you thanks for the opportunity to worship you with others who call you Lord. May I always enter the gates of your sanctuary with praise in my heart and on my lips. Amen.

Week 3: Day 4
The Sacraments of Baptism and Communion

Scripture Reading

Read the following:
- Matthew 26:17-30
- Mark 14:12-26
- Luke 22:7-20
- Acts 2:41-47
- 1 Corinthians 11:17-34

Today's Message

The traditional definition of a *sacrament* is "an outward and visible sign of an inward and spiritual grace."[10] The word sacrament comes from the Latin *sacrare*, which means "to consecrate" or "to make sacred."[11] In the sacraments we assign sacred meaning to ordinary materials. There is nothing inherently special about the substance of the bread and the juice of Communion or the water of baptism except that they are made holy by the faith of the church as Jesus commanded in Scripture.

Like most Protestant churches, The United Methodist Church recognizes two sacraments: baptism and the Lord's Supper. These sacraments mark one's entry into the body of Christ (baptism) and one's ongoing connection to Christ and the community (Communion). To outside observers, what the church does with water, bread, and grape juice can seem baffling. What happens when a baby, child, youth, or adult has water sprinkled on his or her head in front of many people in a church building? Why do people come forward to eat a small piece of bread and drink a sip of juice? What makes these moments meaningful? And why should they be meaningful to you?

We hold the sacraments of baptism and Communion to be critically important to our worship life together because they remind us of the ongoing story of God's love and grace. Just like eating cake and singing "Happy Birthday" draw together vivid memories of the day you were born, the family to which you belong, and your years on earth, so the sacraments of baptism and Communion remind us of our past, the community around us, and our common future. Because of the importance of the sacraments, we will explore each one separately.

Baptism

Jesus defined the mission of the church when he said, "Go therefore and make disciples of all nations, baptizing them in the name of the Father and of the Son and of the Holy Spirit" (Matthew 28:19). United Methodists celebrate baptism in worship because it marks our entry into the body of Christ and affirms our connection with one another. The water symbolizes the grace of God, which cleanses us from sin and gives us a new identity as children of God.[12] More specifically, it symbolizes dying with Christ and being raised to new life with him.

Here are common questions about baptism in The United Methodist Church:

"Why do we baptize babies?"

Infant baptism is the outward and visible sign of the inward and spiritual grace that begins God's work of love in an individual's life before he or she is able to understand it or choose to accept it. Methodists call it "prevenient grace." While some denominations choose to wait until a person is able to couple baptism with understanding and public profession of faith, we invite the parents and the church to affirm this grace on behalf of the child as they pledge to raise the child in the faith until the time that the child is able to accept God's grace for himself or herself, usually at the time of confirmation, which is between sixth and eighth grades in most churches.

We see biblical evidence for God's prevenient grace working in the lives of children when Jesus called the children to come to him, for "it is to such as these that the kingdom of heaven belongs" (Matthew 19:14). Furthermore, entire households were baptized (Acts 16).

Infant baptism also finds its biblical roots in the Old Testament practice of circumcision. Just as Jewish parents took the circumcision vow on behalf of their child, so Christian parents do the same for their children through infant baptism. In both circumcision and baptism, there is an outward sign of an inward grace at work in the child.

The community plays a key role in supporting the child and the family in the faith development of the child, which is articulated in the promises the congregation makes as a part of our baptismal liturgy.

"What happens in baptism?"

When Jesus was baptized, he heard the audible voice of God saying, "You are my Son, the Beloved; with you I am well pleased" (Mark 1:11). We believe that in baptism God speaks that word to every one of us, claiming us as God's own child. We celebrate that gift of God in worship rather than private ceremonies the way families gather for reunions and birthday parties. It is always a cause for the whole spiritual family to celebrate and to remember the meaning of their baptism.

"Why do we use water?"

Throughout Scripture, water is a powerful symbol of God's salvation. In the prayer of thanksgiving over the water, we remember the biblical image of water from creation to the baptism, death, and resurrection of Jesus.[13] Because we practice infant baptism, the most common practice is known as sprinkling, which involves placing a small amount of water on the head of the person being baptized. We also practice baptism by immersion or pouring.

"If I have been baptized, do I have to be baptized again to join The United Methodist Church?"

No. The United Methodist Church believes that baptism is a once-and-for-all-time act of God's grace, whether we remember it or not. To rebaptize would be to deny the way God's grace began a work in your life at some point in the past. If you have been baptized in any Christian denomination, you are invited to reaffirm your baptismal vows when you are received into the church. When the liturgy calls on us to "remember your baptism and be thankful,"[14] we are not simply invited to remember an event in the past, but to remember the way baptism defines who we are and who God has called us to be. Some churches practice a "Reaffirmation of the Baptismal Covenant" in which everyone is invited to recommit themselves to their baptismal vows.

Communion

The second sacrament is Communion—also called the Eucharist or the Lord's Supper. The Gospels recount the story of Jesus' last Passover meal with his disciples on the night before he died. The Apostle Paul defines the meaning of the sacrament in 1 Corinthians 11:17-34.

"Why do we celebrate Communion?"

Holy Communion is a symbolic meal, involving bread and wine—or, more commonly in United Methodist churches, grape juice. It commemorates Jesus' last Passover meal with his disciples on the night before he was crucified. Jesus gave the bread and wine a new significance as symbols of his body and blood, which he was about to sacrifice in his death. He commanded his followers to remember his death by eating bread and drinking wine in his name and promised that he would be with them in this celebration.

"What happens when we take Communion?"

John Wesley included the Lord's Supper as a means of grace and believed that it should be done as often as possible.[15] He asserted that the Lord's Supper is both a converting sacrament and a confirming ordinance of God, which means that God will use it to convert people and to sustain them in their walk with God. It nourishes us as we come to remember Christ's passion, confess our sin, and accept God's grace and forgiveness. It gives us strength and power to be Christ's ambassadors in the world.

"Do the bread and juice actually become the body and blood of Jesus?"

When he instituted Communion, Jesus said of the bread, "This is my body" (Matthew 26:26). He gave them the cup, saying, "This is my blood" (Matthew 26:28). In the Roman Catholic tradition, the bread and wine are believed to actually become Jesus' body and blood (transubstantiation). While there is a range of doctrine among Protestant churches on this issue, United Methodists believe that Christ is present with us in the bread and cup, although they never actually become the body and blood of Christ.

For more about United Methodism's view of the sacrament of Communion, see "This Holy Mystery: A United Methodist Understanding of Holy Communion."[16]

Your Reflections

What are the similarities among Matthew 26:17-30, Mark 14:12-26, and Luke 22:7-20? What are the differences?

What did Paul say to the Corinthians in 1 Corinthians 11:17-34?

How would you explain the meaning of Communion?

Describe a meaningful experience that you have had taking Communion (if applicable).

How would you explain the meaning of baptism?

Have you been baptized? If so, do you have any memories or recollections about your baptism?

If you have not been baptized but plan to do so when you join the church, express what it means to you and why you choose to be baptized.

What questions do you have about Communion and baptism?

(Be sure to share your questions with your group leader and/or contact your pastor.)

Here, O my Lord, I see thee face to face;
here would I touch and handle things unseen;
here grasp with firmer hand eternal grace,
and all my weariness upon thee lean.

Feast after feast thus comes and passes by;
yet, passing, points to the glad feast above,
giving sweet foretaste of the festal joy,
the Lamb's great bridal feast of bliss and love.
—Horatius Bonar[17]

Prayer

Thank you for the gift of your grace, evident through water, bread, and cup. Help me to remember my baptism and connect to Christ's presence in the Lord's Supper. Amen.

Week 3: Day 5
Discipleship Changes as You Grow

Scripture Reading
Read the following:
Hebrews 10:19-25
Philippians 3:7-16

Today's Message
Picture in your imagination the face of your closest friend; someone you have known for a long time; the kind of friend who knows you as well as you know him or her. Now, let's ask a few questions.

- Where did you meet? Who introduced you? What were your first impressions?
- How did the friendship grow? What steps did you take to nurture it?
- What difference has that friendship made in your life?
- How have you changed because of your relationship with this person?

All of us know the way relationships change over time. They begin as an acquaintance—two people who know next to nothing about each other. As times goes by, we get to know each other better by sharing common experiences together. In time, the relationship moves toward a more intimate friendship in which we can be totally open to each other in all of our strengths and weaknesses. Along the way, we both are changed by the influence of the other person in our lives.

In one of the most intimately autobiographical passages of any of his letters, the Apostle Paul said that nothing was more important in his life than knowing Christ. He described his relationship with Christ the way any of us would describe the continued development of the most important friendship in our lives. The apostle was determined to "press on" toward the goal of becoming more and more like the one he followed. He challenged his friends in Philippi to join him in that process (Philippians 3:7-16).

There are many ways of describing the process by which we move in the direction of a life that is centered in loving God and loving others, but because of the inherently relational nature of the gospel, *A Disciple's Path* describes the typical stages along the way in the categories of human relationships (see Week 1). The clear evidence is that being present in Christian community in a small group with other disciples is a critical component of our continued growth toward a Christ-centered life. Let's look at the kind of small-group experience that may be most appropriate for each stage in that process.

Strangers (Ignoring)
If we are honest with ourselves, there is often a time when we ignore the hunger in our souls for a relationship with God. It's not as if we are hostile to God; we just don't seem to need or have time for it. Sometimes it will be through human friendships that we first begin to consider a relationship with Christ.

Acquaintances (Exploring)
If you are at this stage, you may want to engage in a small group that provides an overview of Christian beliefs or the Bible. One example is

Creed: What Christians Believe and Why, by Adam Hamilton (Abingdon Press, 2016). Another option would be to participate in a fellowship group that focuses on building relationships. Often people need to belong before they believe.

Friends (Getting Started)

At this stage in the relationship process, the appropriate form of small-group experience might be a Sunday school class, a short-term Bible study class, or a long-term survey like *Disciple Bible Study* (Abingdon Press).

Good Friends (Going Deeper)

In this stage of spiritual growth, you may want to consider small-group communities that focus on the intentional development of spiritual disciplines. It may also be a time for deeper exploration of the theological foundations of the faith. An example would be *A Disciple's Heart: Growing in Love and Grace* (Abingdon Press, 2015).

Intimate Friendship (Centering on Christ)

As we move into a more intimate relationship with Christ, it may be time to turn from a curriculum-focused small group to a relationship-focused community in which fellow disciples hold one another accountable for their spiritual disciplines. These groups are modeled after the small groups that were at the center of the early Methodist movement. While they still are rooted in biblical study and prayer, these groups become more intimate communities in which people move toward a deeper relationship with Christ and with one another. An example would be the questions John Wesley designed for the small groups at Oxford that became known as the Holy Club.

1. Am I consciously or unconsciously creating the impression that I am better than I am? In other words, am I a hypocrite?
2. Am I honest in all my acts and words, or do I exaggerate?
3. Do I confidentially pass on to another what was told to me in confidence?
4. Can I be trusted?
5. Am I a slave to dress, friends, work or habits?
6. Am I self-conscious, self-pitying, or self-justifying?
7. Did the Bible live in me today?
8. Do I give it time to speak to me every day?
9. Am I enjoying prayer?
10. When did I last speak to someone else about my faith?
11. Do I pray about the money I spend?
12. Do I get to bed on time and get up on time?
13. Do I disobey God in anything?
14. Do I insist upon doing something about which my conscience is uneasy?
15. Am I defeated in any part of my life?
16. Am I jealous, impure, critical, irritable, touchy or distrustful?
17. How do I spend my spare time?
18. Am I proud?
19. Do I thank God that I am not as other people are, especially as the Pharisee who despised the publican?
20. Is there anyone whom I fear, dislike, disown, criticize, hold resentment toward or disregard? If so, what am I doing about it?
21. Do I grumble and complain constantly?
22. Is Christ real to me?[18]

There's no question about it. Asking each other questions like these would be sure to move us toward a deeper, more intimate relationship with Jesus Christ and with one another!

Your Reflections

Review Wesley's twenty-two questions, asking yourself each question.
Write your answers below.

1.

2.

3.

4.

5.

6.

7.

8.

9.

10.

11.

12.

13.

14.

15.

16.

17.

18.

19.

20.

21.

22.

All praise to our redeeming Lord,
who joins us by his grace,
and bids us, each to each restored,
together seek his face.

He bids us build each other up;
and, gathered into one,
to our high calling's glorious hope
we hand in hand go on.

We all partake the joy of one;
the common peace we feel,
a peace to sensual minds unknown,
a joy unspeakable.

And if our fellowship below
in Jesus be so sweet,
what height of rapture shall we know
when round his throne we meet!
—Charles Wesley[19]

Turn now to the Appendix and complete the Small-group Community Profile (page 110).

Prayer

Lord, you designed me to be in relationship with
you and others. Connect me to worship and
fellowship. Guide me to a group of people who
will foster my growth and allow me to participate
in theirs. Amen.

WEEK 4: GIFTS
FINANCIAL GENEROSITY

John Wesley was convinced that there is a direct connection between our discipleship and the use of our financial resources. He called money "an excellent gift of God" and was clear that the "love of money," not money itself, is the "root of all evil." His challenge to the early Methodists was to "gain all you can . . . save all you can . . . and give all you can" as an essential practice of the Christ-centered life.[1] (For an in-depth study of Wesley's teaching on money, see *Earn. Save. Give. Wesley's Simple Rules for Money* (Abingdon Press, 2015).

A biblical understanding of the relationship between our money and our faith begins not in what we do but in what God has done in Jesus Christ. "We love because he first loved us" (1 John 4:19). We give because Jesus gave (Titus 2:14). Our generosity is a finite response to the infinite generosity of God. Followers of Christ find joy in sharing rather than hoarding, giving rather than taking. It is a countercultural way of life that grows in us through the practice of spiritual disciplines that enable us to experience the joy of giving.

This week we focus our attention on the spiritual discipline of financial generosity and the practices that contribute to joyful giving. We will see that Christian generosity is modeled after nothing less than the extravagant generosity of God's love to us in Jesus Christ so that what goes around comes around. It's a circle of generosity. God's generosity to us results in gratitude, which we then express through our generous acts and living. This circle of generosity changes our lives, bringing us to the realization that we are stewards of God's free gifts rather than the owners of what we have.

Week 4: Day 1
It's All God's!

Scripture Reading
Read the following:

Psalm 24:1-2

Matthew 25:14-30

1 Timothy 6:17-19

James 1:17

Today's Message

The Bible has a great deal to say about our financial lives. In fact, Scripture contains more than two thousand references to the subject of money and possessions. Jesus spoke frequently about our use of financial resources. One of the central messages of these Scriptures is that *there is a direct connection between our relationship with money and possessions and our relationship with God.*

Three biblical principles lay the foundation for how we approach the stewardship of our resources as disciples of Jesus Christ:

1) God created everything.
2) God owns everything.
3) As disciples of Jesus, we are not owners of our possessions but trustees of things that belong to God.

Jesus underscored those principles in the story of the rich farmer whose land produced so many crops that he had no place to store them (see Luke 12:14-21). The farmer decided to tear down his old barns and build larger ones in which to store his grain and goods. The self-satisfied, overly stuffed farmer said, "I will say to my soul, Soul, you have ample goods laid up for many years; relax, eat, drink, be merry" (Luke 12:19).

Our culture would call that man a success, but Jesus saw him through the eyes of God, who said, "You fool! This very night your life is being demanded of you. And the things you have prepared, whose will they be?" (verse 20). Jesus concluded, "So it is with those who store up treasures for themselves but are not rich toward God" (verse 21). His warning at the beginning of the story is a warning for all of us: "Take care! Be on your guard against all kinds of greed; for one's life does not consist in the abundance of possessions" (verse 15).

A Christian understanding of the stewardship of our resources begins with the conviction that God entrusted us with financial and physical resources to meet our needs and to enable us to participate in God's redemptive work in the world.

Once we are able to offer God control of our finances, we can offer God our entire lives and experience the spiritual freedom and joy that God intends for us. Wesley's concern was that while "the right use of money" was often considered by what he called "men of the world," it was not given adequate attention by the followers of Christ. The result was that faithful Christian people did not understand how to "employ it to the greatest advantage."[2] For many of us, becoming faithful trustees of our resources can be hindered by the pull of our materialistic culture, a lack of knowledge about wise financial practices, and the need for effective tools to implement those practices. So, where do we begin?

Episcopal priest and author Gerald Keucher gives this sound advice:

If you really want your heart to be with God . . . then you might want to change how you give to your [church] and to

God's work accomplished by other charities. Don't treat your charitable giving as just another bill that has to be paid—or as one that doesn't get paid if there's not enough left over. Don't think of your gift as a tax or as club dues, and for heaven's sake, don't let it be just a tip that's less than you spend on lunches or commuting.

Make your gift a first-fruits offering. Fix a percentage in your heart and in your head, and give that percentage off the top to God every time money goes into your bank or into your hand.[3]

Keucher goes on to explain that the biblical percentage is 10 percent, but that giving God any percentage off the top is "better for your heart" than giving any amount that is not off the top and has no relationship to your income.

The important first step is recognizing that all we have comes from God and belongs to God. From there we can begin to give of what we have with a heart of gratitude.

Your Reflections

Do you see a connection between your relationship with money and your relationship with God? If yes, say more about that. If not, why not?

Do you believe that God owns everything? Why or why not?

Do you believe your money comes from God and belongs to God?

"An excellent branch of Christian wisdom is . . . namely, the right use of money—a subject largely spoken of, after their manner, by men of the world; but not sufficiently considered by those whom God hath chosen out of the world."

—John Wesley[4]

If yes, how do you respond to that belief? In other words, how have you been a trustee of God's financial resources in your life?

Are you giving of what you have with a heart of gratitude?

What has changed in your relationship with God and money over time?

Prayer

"Who am I, and what is my people, that we should be able to make this freewill offering? For all things come from you, and of your own have we given you. For we are aliens and transients before you, as were all our ancestors; our days on the earth are like a shadow, and there is no hope. O LORD our God, all this abundance that we have provided for building you a house for your holy name comes from your hand and is all your own. I know, my God, that you search the heart, and take pleasure in uprightness; in the uprightness of my heart I have freely offered all these things" (1 Chronicles 29:14-17).

Week 4: Day 2
The Tithe

Scripture Reading
Read the following:
    Matthew 23:23-24
    Matthew 6:1-4, 19-21

Today's Message
How do you feel when you hear the word *tithe?* What do you think?

The Old Testament talks frequently about the tithe—the first 10 percent of one's earnings, harvest, or other resources. The people were to give a tithe to God, and they were to do it with gratitude.

Let's consider a simple explanation of the Old Testament practice of tithing. Review the following Bible passages:

1. Numbers 18:21: The people paid a general tithe to the Levites.
2. Numbers 18:25-31: The Levites paid a portion of the general tithe to the priests.
3. Deuteronomy 14:22-27: The people kept a tithe to pay for their annual pilgrimage to Jerusalem.
4. Deuteronomy 14:28-29: The people paid a tithe for the poor, the orphans, and the widows.

The Levites were one of the twelve tribes of Israel. The Levites worked for Israel, and in return for their work, they received 10 percent from the rest of the population. All priests were Levites, yet not all Levites were priests. The priests took care of all the responsibilities associated with the temple. If possible, all people were to take an annual pilgrimage to Jerusalem and provide a tithe at that time. And every three years, the Israelites gave a tithe for the poor, the orphans, and the widows.

Next Sunday, pay attention during worship and listen for these or similar words: "We offer God's tithes and our gifts and offerings." This declaration has been the tradition of the church for as long as its history. The people of God—you and me—give to the church because of our gratitude to the Lord. We give back to God what is God's so that through our gifts the love of God can become a tangible reality in our world. This time of giving in worship is a reminder of the blessings God gives us and gave to us through Jesus Christ.

So, what did Jesus think about the tithe? Jesus probably did not have to teach people to tithe; in his time the tithe was a given. But Jesus stressed that giving was about the condition of the heart. It was about giving from desire and not from the legalistic requirement of the law. Getting in a right relationship with God was about the inner heart, not the outer actions.

We respond to the abundance of God in the form of our prayers, our presence in worship together, our financial gifts to support the church, our service as a part of the body of Christ, and our witness to others who have not yet experienced Christ. It is the whole of our lives—our time, resources, and attention—directed to God. Our tithe goes to the church to support God's kingdom work and mission—to make disciples who participate in God's transformation of the world. As Christians, we support the church and other Christian causes so that God's love is tangibly experienced in this world. Healing cannot take place without it.

To conclude today's reading, let's review frequently asked questions about giving and the tithe.

"How much should I give?"

That's between you and God. The biblical pattern of tithing is giving the first 10 percent of your income to God as a practical discipline for spiritual growth (see Malachi 3:8-12). Some people begin with a smaller percentage and grow into the tithe. Those who are already giving 10 percent often feel God calling them to give beyond the tithe as their faith and discipleship continue to grow. Everyone is challenged to take the next step in giving.

"Should the tithe be based on my gross income or my net income after taxes?"

Again, everyone must seek God's direction in his or her giving decisions. Traditional interpretations indicate the biblical tithe represents the firstfruits of our income. By giving before the costs of housing, transportation, taxes, and other expenses, we honor the principle that God owns everything and we can joyfully trust God to allow us to live fully on the other 90 percent.

"Will I be expected to tithe?"

The biblical practice of offering 10 percent of our income to God is a valuable spiritual discipline. It can make a big difference in our lives and is a biblical expectation for committed disciples of Christ. Although no one in the church tells anyone else how much to give, the expectation of our membership vows is that we will share in the financial support of the church's ministry.

"Is my salvation determined by the level of my giving?"

No. We are saved by God's grace. Salvation is a free gift accepted by faith. But living into that salvation—what we call the discipleship path—includes learning how to use the gifts that God gives us so that our whole life is shaped and formed around our salvation and our gifts can be used as a part of God's work of salvation in the world.

"If I do not tithe, am I still welcome in the church?"

Absolutely. Tithing is a personal, spiritual discipline. The United Methodist denomination welcomes everyone who comes to experience God's love in Christ, regardless of where he or she is on the spiritual journey.

"Where can I find help with my finances and find ways to give?"

Many congregations offer small-group studies or classes on stewardship, financial management, budgeting, and estate planning. If these resources are not available in your local congregation, you may find information in your district or conference offices.

Now read Malachi 3:8-12 and use SOAPY or *Lectio Divina* (see pages 45-47). Record your notes from the experience below:

Your Reflections

What does the Bible teach us about tithing?

How do you feel when you hear the word *tithe*?

What is your current practice of giving?

What is your next step toward growth in your giving?

> "If those who 'gain all they can' and 'save all they can' will likewise 'give all they can' then, the more they gain the more they will grow in grace, and the more treasure they will lay up in heaven."
>
> —John Wesley[5]

Prayer

Lord, Giver of all things, I recognize and praise you for your creation. Thank you for the abilities, talents, resources, and life that you have created in and through me. May I be grateful and have wisdom to know how to be a steward of those resources to support my family, the church, and the needs of the world. Give me direction and wisdom related to tithing. May I know the knowledge of your will and have the power to carry it out. Amen.

WEEK 4: DAY 3
CHEERFUL GIVER

Scripture Reading
Read the following:
   2 Corinthians 8:1-5
   2 Corinthians 9:1-15

Today's Message

Have you ever heard the term *cheerful giver*? How many cheerful givers do you know? Do you think giving away stuff, including money, creates joy? Why does it seem that when we give something out of love, we feel different—even joyful?

Recall a moment when you gave money to a cause or group you believed would do good for someone or something. What about it gave you joy? From where did this joy emerge?

That's the kind of joy God calls us to have as we support the church to accomplish God's mission in the world. We grow spiritually as we begin to allow God to reorder our priorities to kingdom priorities. Giving cheerfully emerges from an attitude of gratitude, not from a spirit of fear or scarcity.

In 2 Corinthians 9:7, the Apostle Paul tells us that we should give cheerfully. Paul was writing to the more well-off church of Corinth, and he lifted the example of the poor Christians in Macedonia (2 Corinthians 8) to stir the hearts of the Christians in Corinth.

Luke 21:1-4 shows the way that Jesus defined generosity—not by the size of the gift, but by the condition of the heart from which it is given. For Jesus, motivation seemed to be everything.

Motivation *is* everything.

You may be familiar with John 3:16, but have you ever thought about this verse in relationship to fiscal giving or to God's mission to make disciples and transform the world? The passage says, "For God so loved the world that He gave His only begotten Son, that whoever believes in Him should not perish but have everlasting life" (NKJV). God's giving has to be the very foundation of our giving. Notice three things about God's giving through Jesus:

1. God's motivation was love.
2. God gave God's own Son.
3. God's giving was in response to our need—that we "should not perish."

God looks at the motivation of your heart and is not impressed or pleased by loveless giving. The only form of sacrificial giving that God does not seem to appreciate is sacrificial giving without love: "If I give all I possess to the poor and surrender my body to the flames, *but have not love,* I gain nothing" (1 Corinthians 13:3 NIV, emphasis added).

We are to give cheerfully, in response to need, and from a motivation of love.

Now read John 3:16 and use SOAPY or *Lectio Divina* (see pages 45-47). Record your notes from the experience below:

Your Reflections

Why is giving a matter of the heart, and why does giving cheerfully matter?

Do you believe that the motivation behind our generosity really matters to God? Why or why not?

What is the relationship between our giving and God's mission to make disciples of the world?

What difference would the discipline of tithing make in your life and in the ministry of the church?

What blessings have resulted from your willingness to give?

Prayer

God, you are the Giver of all good things. Teach us to give not out of guilt or fear or mere obligation, but out of a spirit of joy and freedom, knowing that as we learn to give of our means to you, we can give our whole lives to you. Amen.

> "It is the preacher's job not to tell people what to do, but rather to remind them who they are, in this instance, agents, or stewards, of God's bounty. . . . The goal of Christianity is not detachment from material wealth, but the loving use of it."
>
> —William Sloane Coffin[6]

> "When a believer gives all of life to God, the use of money is no longer a decision made by the believer alone. Once this transaction of faith has taken place, the use of money is at the direction of God and faithfulness demands obedience to that direction. . . . To follow Wesley's example is to begin to transform the world through the appropriate use of the money placed in our hands by God."
>
> —Rueben Job[7]

WEEK 4: DAY 4
IT'S THE HEART, NOT THE SIZE

Scripture Reading

Read the following:
Mark 12:41-44
Luke 12:42-48
Luke 21:1-4

Now read Acts 20:32-35 and use SOAPY or *Lectio Divina* (see pages 45-47). Record your notes from the experience below:

Today's Message

Yesterday we considered the idea of giving cheerfully out of a motivation of love, acknowledging that the condition of the heart, not the size of the gift, is what is important.

The story of the widow's offering points to the heart's disposition in giving rather than to the size of the gift. Apparently rich people were dropping obviously large gifts in the offering boxes in the temple. Then a very poor widow—who would have been at the bottom of society—gave a small amount, but it was everything that she had. Jesus highlighted her gift, saying that it was greater than all the others because it reflected the condition of her heart. Like the widow, we are called to give humbly and discreetly according to what we have, trusting that God knows our motivation and desire.

Jesus warned the disciples to beware of practicing righteousness before others in order to be noticed. He said,

> Whenever you give alms [or tithe], do not sound a trumpet before you, as the hypocrites do in the synagogues [churches] and in the streets, so that they may be praised by others. Truly I tell you, they have received their reward. But when you give alms, do not let your left hand know what your right hand is doing, so that your alms may be done in secret; and your Father who sees in secret will reward you. (Matthew 6:2-4)

The same can be said for us. We are to give in secret so that our egos, which want attention and praise, can be left out of it.

Jesus also encouraged generous giving. The widow's gift may not have made a big difference in the temple budget, but it made a huge difference in the life of the woman who gave it. Like the widow, we are to give according to what we have been given. Jesus said, "From everyone to whom much has been given, much will be required" (Luke 12:48).

There is no room for comparison when it comes to giving. We give different sums of money to support God's kingdom work. Some of us give larger amounts, and some of us give smaller amounts. What matters is not so much the size of the gift in terms of its impact on others, but the size of the gift in terms of its impact on the giver. The question to ask yourself is, *What is the condition of my heart?*

Your Reflections

What does giving sacrificially mean to you?

How can you give sacrificially like the widow? What changes might you need to make?

Why is giving secretly and with humility important?

Prayer

Lord, help me to give sacrificially to provide for the ministry of the church. Help me to give out of a humble and pure heart. Guide me in the area of my finances. I offer them to you. Amen.

> "You do not consider, money never stays with me; it would burn me if it did. I throw it out of my hands as soon as possible, lest it should find a way, into my heart."
> —John Wesley[8]

WEEK 4: DAY 5
10-10-80

Scripture Reading
Read the following:
    Matthew 25:14-30
    Proverbs 3:9
    Proverbs 11:24-28

Today's Message

The Bible makes it clear that God calls us to order our financial lives around our commitment to Christ. Getting our financial lives in order takes time, intention, knowledge of wise financial practices, a plan, and effective tools to implement the plan. It is not only about giving to the church so that God's plans can be fulfilled; it also involves getting our financial lives in order.

Let's be honest. We live in a consumer-driven society built upon producing and consuming goods and services. Our culture tells us that to be happy or fulfilled, we must consume continually and go into debt. Instant gratification is the norm rather than the exception. More and more, bigger and better—that is the pull of a materialistic culture. Our culture is based upon materialism, yet this seems to run counter to the Christian journey. To some degree, all of us participate in it, but is there another way? We believe there is, and it involves another essential spiritual practice of the discipleship pathway: budgeting.

Today we would like to suggest a plan to help you get your financial life in order using the 10-10-80 principle:

• Give the first 10 percent to God.
• Save the next 10 percent for the future.
• Live on 80 percent of your income.

Sound radical? Maybe in our times, but those who use this plan can testify to how it enables them to be faithful to biblical principles and how they have experienced freedom in their lives. God does not want anything to own us; moving toward and growing into 10-10-80 living help us rely on God and achieve financial freedom from the bondage of materialism.

For some of us, the financial discipline of giving is very new. We want to know where to start.

Our suggestion is to start somewhere. Pray about it and listen to what God is calling you to give—but start *somewhere*. God will guide you as you pray about your decision. Here are practical steps to follow in the process:

• **Assess where you are.** Determine the percentage of income you give away. How much do you give yearly to the church? To other charitable organizations? Divide each figure by your gross income to get the percentage you give to church and the percentage you give to other charitable organizations. For example, if you make $50,000 and give $500 a year to your faith community, you give 1 percent of your income to the church. If you give another $500 to charitable organizations, you give an additional 1 percent of your income, and your total giving equals 2 percent of your income.

• **Review your income, expenses, and priorities.** Explore the way your budget reflects the priorities in your life, remembering that Jesus said, "Where your treasure is, there will your heart be also" (Matthew 6:21). Does the way you use your money bear witness to the things you think are most important to you?

• **Pick a percentage.** Determine to give God a percentage of what God has given you. Many people begin with 2 or 3 percent of their income and grow toward the goal of tithing. Whatever percentage God directs you to give, determine to give this percentage off the top, which brings you to the final step.

• **Make your gift a firstfruits offering.** Decide to give the percentage you determined every time you receive income—whether it goes into the bank or into your hand. If you are paid biweekly, give biweekly. If you are paid once a month, then give your percentage off the top once a month, and don't give the other weeks. If you are paid twice a month or every other week, then give at those times. This is the first radical step because it makes you think about what you have been given and how you will give back. Give to God at those times when God has given you something.

Ultimately, giving assists God in accomplishing the Great Commission:

> Therefore, go and make disciples of all the nations, baptizing them in the name of the Father and the Son and the Holy Spirit.

Teach these new disciples to obey all the commands I have given you. And be sure of this: I am with you always, even to the end of the age.(Matthew 28:19-20 NLT)

As followers of Christ in The United Methodist Church, when we give to support our local congregation, we also share in the global ministries of The United Methodist Church, touching the lives of people of all ages all around the world. Our gifts, in connection with the gifts of other United Methodist disciples, enable us to participate in the mission of making disciples of Jesus Christ for the transformation of the world. (For more information on the connectional ministries in which your congregation shares, contact your conference office or go to www.umc.org.)

Your Reflections
Write your thoughts about the 10-10-80 principle below:

> "It is true, riches, and the increase of them, are the gift of God. Yet great care is to be taken, that what is intended for a blessing, do not turn into a curse."
> —John Wesley[9]

What percentage of your income do you give to the church each month?

What percentage of your income do you save each month?

What percentage of your income do you spend each month?

How close are you to ordering your finances according to the 10-10-80 principle?

not close   **getting there**   **I'm there**

What steps will you take to move toward the 10-10-80 model?

Circle your current level of giving to the church.

never give   **give sporadically**   **regularly give percentage**

regularly tithe   **moving beyond the tithe**

In your own words, how would you explain the biblical discipline of tithing?

What questions about tithing do you have?

What could be your next step toward growth in the practice of financial generosity?
What percentage of your income will you commit to give to God?

Prayer

Lord, order my steps and my heart. You know everything about me and within me. Search my heart, and show me where and how to grow in my giving. Help me order my financial life around you and your priorities. Amen.

Week 5: Service
Spiritual Gifts and Gifts-based Service

Jesus' disciples were shocked. None of them expected what happened when they gathered in that upper room to celebrate the Passover. Jesus washed their feet (John 13:1-20)!

Foot washing was the common practice of hospitality in the dusty, dry Middle Eastern culture where people generally wore sandals. The host would provide water for a servant to wash the weary, dirty feet of the guests—or for the guests to wash their own feet.

That's what the disciples expected, but when they arrived in the upper room, there was no servant to wash their feet. They were shocked when Jesus—their rabbi, leader, and host of the dinner—got up from the table, took off his robe, wrapped a towel around his waist, picked up the towel and basin, knelt in front of them, and began washing their feet. The Son of God was doing the work of a servant, washing his disciples' feet. No wonder Peter resisted him.

Can you sense just how radical Jesus' action was? In that act, the incarnate God showed us the nature of servanthood. John Ortberg writes, "God is the Infinite Servant. . . . Jesus did not come as a servant *in spite of* the fact that he is God; he came *precisely because* of the fact that he is God."[1] What was even more shocking was hearing Jesus say, "You call me Teacher and Lord—and you are right, for that is what I am. So if I, your Lord and Teacher, have washed your feet, you also ought to wash one another's feet. For I have set you an example, that you also should do as I have done to you" (John 13:13-15).

This week we will explore servanthood—the practice by which the love of God becomes a tangible reality in our lives and through which we become active participants in God's transformation of the world. Through our baptism, we are commissioned to use our gifts to continue the servant ministry of Jesus. Each disciple has a role in the body of Christ. Every disciple is called, gifted, and needed in the ministry of the church. You will explore how God has gifted you, where your heart has been broken, and where you are called to serve. The intent is that this exploration will assist you in finding your gifts and your calling as a servant of Jesus Christ.

"I don't know what your destiny will be, but one thing I know: the only ones among you who will be really happy are those who have sought and found how to serve."
—Albert Schweitzer[2]

Week 5: Day 1
Priesthood of All Believers

Scripture Reading

Read the following:

1 Peter 4:8-11

1 Peter 2:4-10

Choose one of the above passages and use SOAPY or *Lectio Divina* (see pages 45-47). Record notes about your experience below:

Today's Message

It may come as a surprise to discover that you are a *minister*.

The writer of the epistle named for Peter identifies followers of Christ as "a chosen race, a royal priesthood, a holy nation" (1 Peter 2:9). One of the primary affirmations of the Protestant Reformation is the priesthood of all believers. The *Discipline* declares that "all Christians are called through their baptism to this ministry of servanthood in the world to the glory of God and for human fulfillment."[3]

You are a minister. As a follower of Christ, you are called to active participation in Christ's ministry of service in the world, whether you are a clergy person, church staff member, or layperson; a man, woman, or child; a person who knows the Bible well or one who knows the Bible hardly at all. All of us are called, and that includes you! If you are a layperson (not ordained clergy), you are not just a volunteer who works in the church. You are called by God and equipped by the Spirit to serve as Christ has served in places where you find the greatest joy and deepest connection to God and God's people. God calls us all to serve so that the body of Christ fulfills its calling in this world.

Some persons are called to ordination. This is the process by which individuals are set apart to lead the church in its ministry of witness and service. In The United Methodist Church, these persons are ordained to word, sacrament, and order as elders, or to ministries of love, justice, and service as deacons. However, those who are not called to ordination are not off the hook!

Every follower of Christ has been given spiritual gifts to fulfill God's calling for his or her servanthood. Our individual calling is always a part of God's mission for the church. We cannot fulfill our individual calling without being a part of the Christian community.

God has wired you to fulfill your ministry of servanthood. The church's task is to help you discover your gifts and find your place to serve, and then to support you in it. We will focus on the discovery of our spiritual gifts tomorrow. For today, you are invited to consider what it means to be a servant of Jesus Christ as you respond to the call to participate in God's transformation of the world.

Your Reflections

What do you think about being identified as part of a "royal priesthood"?

How does it feel to hear that you are called to ministry as a disciple of Jesus?

How have you experienced some awareness of this calling in your life?

What are the ways that you serve others now—formally and informally?

> "The laity had come to see, with a shock, that they were the front line soldiers of the Church. They, not the clergy, were the representatives of Christ who were actually present in the factories, shops, offices, schools and homes of the country. If Christ's compassion was to get into those situations, then they, the laity, must be the channels through which it would come. If Christ's truth was to be spoken, then they must speak it."
>
> —Stephen Verney[4]

Prayer

Lord, I pray that you might reveal your purpose for me and show me the path that you want me to take. Please show me with clarity the gifts that you have given me to share with others. In Jesus' name. Amen.

Week 5: Day 2
Spiritual Gifts

Scripture Reading
Read the following:
> Romans 12:1-8
> 1 Corinthians 12:1-31
> Ephesians 4:1-16

Today's Message

What does it mean for you to give or receive a gift? Gifts are often given on special occasions to mark significant events: birthdays, Christmas, Easter, anniversaries, graduations, or personal accomplishments. In these cases, most gifts are intended for personal use or individual enjoyment. We accept the gift with appreciation and without expectation. Usually we feel obligated to thank the giver through a kind word or thank you card, but we are not necessarily obliged to reciprocate.

Sometimes we refer to gifts as unique talents. We may say that a person is gifted in music, sports, or leadership, meaning that he or she has a special aptitude for a specific task.

While the New Testament description of spiritual gifts has some similarities to this understanding of gifts, there are other ways in which they are unique:

- Spiritual gifts are gifts of grace given to followers of Christ, not by some accomplishment of their own.
- Spiritual gifts are given by God, and recipients have a responsibility to use them for the greatest good of the ministry of Christ's body in the world.
- God has prewired us to use our natural talents, personalities, gifts, and passions to become a part of God's transformation of the world by the power of the Holy Spirit.

In his first letter to the Corinthians, the Apostle Paul tells us that there are a variety of gifts but all come from the same Spirit. Every spiritual gift is equally important. As a part of the universal body of Christ, you have an integral role to fulfill. Gifts are given not to be left idle but to be used in community to serve God and others. Every person's gifts are necessary for the church to fulfill its mission of making disciples for the transformation of the world. As we discover our gifts and release those gifts for servant ministry, we grow in our love of God and our love for others and find our unique place in God's work of transformation in the world.

In "Your Reflections," you will be instructed to use an online spiritual gifts assessment. There are no correct answers. It is not a test. You cannot fail. Because you do not score highly in one area does not necessarily mean that you do not have that gift; it means that this gift may not be the way that God plans to use you in the church. The purpose of the assessment is to give you an indicator of the spiritual gifts that Christ *could* have given you. The confirmation of gifts comes through the experience of serving and in receiving the affirmation of other disciples who serve alongside you. So, just because the assessment indicates a number of gifts, it may not mean you are called to use all of them.

Often when people take the assessment, they will score high on three or four spiritual gifts. That may mean that the person ought to try a service role that fits with one or more of those gifts as a way of confirming his or her gift through service.

This assessment is a map or a guide, not an authority. It can provide direction regarding how and where God might be calling you to serve the church for the purpose of creating healing in the world and building the body of Christ. As you begin to identify your spiritual gifts, keep these things in mind:

• You have been given at least one spiritual gift for God's purpose.
• Spiritual gifts are different from, although not contradictory to, your natural talents.
• The role of the church is to help you discover your gifts and find a place to use them.
• No one gift is more important than another. Every gift matters.

• Your spiritual gift is to be used to accomplish God's mission in the world. In a real sense, it is your responsibility to glorify God and to give your gift back to the one who gave it.
• Our gifts and calling are confirmed in community with other disciples.
• The discovery and use of our gifts always results in joy for us and in blessing for others.

Your Reflections
In the space below, write the gifts listed in Romans 12, 1 Corinthians 12, and Ephesians 4. Then write your thoughts about spiritual gifts in general.

"Each gift is an invitation and provides the means to participate in the work of Jesus. . . . These are gifts that equip us to work alongside of and in company with Jesus. . . . We are being invited into a working relationship in the operations of the Trinity."
—Eugene Peterson[5]

Review the Spiritual Gifts Overview and Spiritual Gifts Descriptions found in the Appendix (pages 116-21). Prior to taking the online spiritual gifts assessment, identify the three gifts listed in the Spiritual Gifts Overview that you think best describe you. Write those three gifts below.

1. _____ 2. _____ 3. _____

Now, without indicating what you think your gifts are, ask a friend, spouse, or relative to review the Spiritual Gifts Overview and tell you the three gifts he or she thinks you have. Write them here:

1. _____ 2. _____ 3. _____

Finally, take the spiritual gifts assessment found at http://survey.adultbiblestudies.com/.

List below your top three spiritual gifts.

1. _____ 2. _____ 3. _____

Did you have any surprises after taking the assessment? If so, what are they?

Write about how you think God might use your gifts in ministry.

Prayer

Lord, I pray for your wisdom, discernment, and guidance as I seek to identify the spiritual gift(s) you have given me. I humbly ask for understanding so that I may use my gift(s) to share your love with others. Amen.

Week 5: Day 3
Servanthood

Scripture Reading

Read the following:
- John 13:12-17
- Philippians 2:1-11
- Ephesians 4:12

Now read James 1:22-25, 27 and use SOAPY or *Lectio Divina* (see pages 45-47). Record notes about your experience here:

Today's Message

We began this week with Jesus' disciples in the upper room. With them, we were amazed at the model of servanthood we experienced in watching Jesus wash their feet. We return there today to consider the difference between being a *servant* and a *volunteer*. One of the goals of *A Disciple's Path* is to move us from a volunteer mentality to a servant mentality.

The word *volunteer* means different things to different people, but it is not a word we find in the Bible. The New Testament word is *servant*. Without depreciating the importance of volunteering, it is helpful to point out some differences between being a volunteer and being a servant:

- Being a volunteer describes a particular activity that is not at the center of one's identity, whereas being a servant describes something about who one is as a follower of Jesus Christ.
- Generally speaking, a volunteer gives of time and talent when it is convenient or when it fits one's schedule, whereas a disciple of Jesus Christ knows that he or she is a servant all the time.
- A volunteer serves on the basis of his or her interests and values, whereas a servant is guided by the values of the kingdom of God revealed in Jesus Christ.

From the beginning of this journey, we've seen that being a disciple of Jesus Christ involves more than simply growing in knowledge and belief. It also involves action. As we move along the path of discipleship, we are inspired to serve in tangible ways to bring about God's transformation of the world. Our faith and our service are intrinsically bound together.

The writer of the epistle of James emphasized the inescapable connection between our faith and our works.

> *What good is it, my brothers and sisters, if you say you have faith but do not have works? Can faith save you? If a brother or sister is naked and lacks daily food, and one of you says to them, "Go in peace; keep warm and eat your fill,"*

and yet you do not supply their bodily needs, what is the good of that? So faith by itself, if it has no works, is dead. (James 2:14-17)

Faith without works is dead. What we believe is directly connected with what we do. As we serve in community, we grow in our faith; and as we grow in our faith, we learn to serve. Belief is like breathing in; serving is like breathing out. Stop doing either one of them and we die. In serving out of our spiritual gifts, we grow into the likeness of Jesus, the Servant, and share in God's saving work in the world.

A primary role of the church is to train its members for ministry. In his letter to the Ephesians, the Apostle Paul says that church leaders are called to "equip the saints for the work of ministry, for the building up of the body of Christ" (Ephesians 4:12). The Greek word for *equip* is a medical term that describes the setting of a dislocated joint. It comes from a root word used to describe mending and repairing nets. It also can mean "to make fit" for a task. It paints a picture of the way the spirit of God works through the church to mend or fix the broken places in our lives so that we become whole, healthy, and fit for ministry.

The pathway of discipleship leads us from a self-centered life to a Christ-centered life, from brokenness to wholeness, from apathy to compassion, from hearing to doing, from passive belief to energetic action. Along the way, we discover that God has gifted us for servanthood in the body of Christ. In community with other disciples, we are made fit for ministry by the power of the spirit of God.

Forth in thy name, O Lord, I go,
my daily labor to pursue;
thee, only thee, resolved to know
in all I think or speak or do.

The task thy wisdom hath assigned,
O let me cheerfully fulfill;
in all my works thy presence find,
and prove thy good and perfect will.

For thee delightfully employ
what e'er thy bounteous grace hath given;
and run my course with even joy,
and closely walk with thee to heaven.

—Charles Wesley[6]

Your Reflections

What does Christ's humility communicate to you about servanthood? About the nature of God?

How have you observed the differences between being a volunteer and being a servant?

Would you say that you are both a hearer of the word and a doer of the word? Why or why not?

How have you seen the body of Christ equipping people for servant ministry?

What positive experiences have you had in using your gifts, talents, and/or abilities to make a real difference in someone else's life—with no expectation of return?

Describe the most positive serving/volunteer experience you have had (in church or elsewhere). How did you see God working in and through you?

Prayer
Lord, you humbled yourself and became a servant to show us the way of self-giving love. Teach us the way of servanthood that we might become the agents of your saving love in this world. Amen.

Week 5: Day 4
The Body of Christ and Ways of Serving

Scripture Reading

Read 1 Corinthians 12:18-27 and use SOAPY or *Lectio Divina* (see pages 45-47). Record notes about your experience below:

Today's Message

How does God get God's work done in this world? Jesus taught his disciples to pray for God's kingdom to come and God's will to be done on earth as it is done in heaven, but how does it happen? How does God's kingdom come? How does God's will get done here, on earth, among people like us?

The surprising answer is that God's primary means for getting God's saving work done is through the church, which the Apostle Paul called "the body of Christ." Just as God was present in Jesus, so the risen Christ continues to be present in this world through the always human, amazingly diverse, often imperfect, sometimes disobedient body called "church."

If Paul's words seem a little hard for you to believe, you may understand an old Irish toast that says:

> *To live above with the Saints we love,*
> *Ah, that is the purest glory.*
> *To live below with the Saints we know,*
> *Ah, that is another story![7]*

There is no such thing as a perfect church, largely because there are no perfect disciples. The best Paul could say was that "we have this treasure in clay jars, so that it may be made clear that this extraordinary power belongs to God and does not come from us" (2 Corinthians 4:7).

And yet, in spite of its imperfections, God has not given up on the church. God's love continues to become a reality in this world through the lives of ordinary followers of Christ who continue to grow into a life in which they love God with their whole hearts, souls, minds, and strength and learn to love others the way Jesus loved them. God continues to call the church to be the primary means by which God is at work to transform the kingdoms of this earth into the kingdom of God.

To be more specific, God intends for the congregation of which you are a part to be the tangible expression of Christ's presence in your community. As a follower of Jesus, you are called to be one of the persons through whom the risen Christ is alive in this world. The apostle wrote, "Now you are the body of Christ and individually members of it" (1 Corinthians 12:27). You are part of the body of Christ, and you have a role to play. You are called to serve.

Finding a Place to Serve

A Disciple's Path is designed primarily to help individual disciples find their place to serve in their local congregation of that part of the body of Christ known as The United Methodist Church. Consider where you might participate according to your giftedness. At the end of this study, you will be encouraged to make some decisions about your next steps in the disciplines of daily prayer and reflection on Scripture, worship and small-group community, financial giving, gifts-based service, and witness. These disciplines form us in God's likeness and image. As we engage together to live a life that centers on loving

Christ and loving others, we begin to accomplish God's mission of bringing healing and wholeness to a suffering world. Engaging in your faith community and the surrounding community is foundational to making that happen. When people do not engage, the faith community is incomplete and cannot function at its best. Additionally, some part of bringing healing does not happen when every member is not engaged. You are a vital part of the church's mission.

If your faith community has a catalog or descriptive listing of ministry opportunities, take it out now and review it. (Your leader should have provided this at the end of group session 4.) Or find information about ministry opportunities on your church website. Read about things that interest you. Think about your spiritual gifts and what your role might be in the body of Christ. Commit to pray about it for the remainder of the week. Think about the church and the roles in which you see people serving. If you are already serving, ask yourself, *Am I serving out of my giftedness? Do I love what I am doing? Do I feel God's work in and through me?*

Your Reflections

Are you currently serving in the church?
If so, are you serving out of your giftedness?

Do you love what you are doing? Do you feel God's work in and through you?

If the answer to any of the above questions is no, what step might you take to move toward serving out of your giftedness?

Christ, from whom all blessings flow,
perfecting the saints below,
hear us, who thy nature share,
who thy mystic body are.

Join us, in one spirit join,
let us still receive of thine;
still for more on thee we call,
thou who fillest all in all.

Move and actuate and guide,
diverse gifts to each divide;
placed according to thy will,
let us all our work fulfill;

Love, like death, hath all destroyed,
rendered all distinctions void;
names and sects and parties fall;
thou, O Christ, art all in all!
—Charles Wesley[8]

Prayer

God, you are the Giver of all good gifts. We pray for knowledge of your will and the power to carry it out by serving others in your name. Amen.

Week 5: Day 5
Divine Discontent

Scripture Reading
Read the following:
> Exodus 3:1-13
> Matthew 25:31-46

Today's Message

What's your passion? The word *passion* can mean different things. It can be used to describe an interest. It can mean fervor, obsession, infatuation, excitement, enthusiasm, gusto, zeal, and zest. People can have a passion for food, sports, painting, gardening, knitting, cars, or just about anything.

Passions and interests are wonderful parts of human experience and should be nurtured and encouraged. They bring excitement and joy to our lives. But when we talk about passion in the context of spiritual gifts, we mean something a little different. This kind of passion is a God-given desire to help in healing a broken world. The prophet Jeremiah described it as "a burning fire shut up in my bones" (Jeremiah 20:9). He was weary holding it in, but he could hold it no longer.

A spiritual passion is a relentless longing for justice— the prophetic calling to make wrong things right. It's the kind of Spirit-implanted passion that caused some of the most well-known biblical figures to take action because they were moved by the needs of the people around them:

- Moses eventually became a liberator after seeing the injustice of his people in slavery (Exodus 2:1-15).
- Esther put her life on the line when her people were threatened with extermination (Esther 4:1-17).
- David stepped into battle when he saw a giant threatening his country (1 Samuel 17:1-58).

You may think that your calling would never equal these, but God has an odd way of calling people who do not think they are worthy. God calls us in the context of our experience to become a part of something bigger than we could ever imagine.

As followers of Jesus, we follow a Master who was moved with compassion when he saw the crowds who were like sheep without a shepherd (Matthew 9:36), when he confronted their sickness (Matthew 14:14), and when he saw that they had nothing to eat (Matthew 15:32). That same compassion burns in the hearts of Jesus' followers when we realize that things in the world just aren't right. When we see a need that cries out to be addressed, the spirit of God sparks a fire in our bones, an itch that must be scratched, a deep inner desire to heal things that are broken. It is an expression of the "divine discontent" that begins with our hunger for God and results in a desire to meet the needs of others.

Sometimes we recognize our discontent but ignore it, or we tell ourselves that we will engage the issue when we are less busy. But if it is a calling that God has instilled within our hearts, it doesn't go away. If nothing breaks your heart, you might not be paying attention. Start praying, and ask God to show you your divine discontent.

Remember that not every problem or societal need is yours to tackle, but don't give up too soon. Discovery is a process. It usually involves confirmation from other Christians. When you receive clarity about your calling, a first step might be to increase your exposure to the issue. For example, if your heart breaks for abused children, spend an afternoon at a shelter for abused kids. Exposure to the right issue will ignite the Holy Spirit to fuel your passion! For an in-depth study of this theme, see *Make a Difference: Following Your Passion and Finding Your Place to Serve* (Abingdon Press, 2017).

Now read Ephesians 2:10 and use SOAPY or *Lectio Divina* (see pages 45-47). Record notes about your experience here:

Your Reflections
Write your thoughts and reflections about the texts from today's Scripture Reading.

"Unlike some forms of Christianity, the goal of which seems to be the redemption of one's own soul, the ultimate goal of Wesleyanism is the redemption of the other and the world. . . . Our charge is to glorify God, and we do so most fully by becoming the servants of all. . . . The genuine Christian is the one who embraces the mission of Jesus in humility and servanthood."
—Paul Wesley Chilcote[9]

What breaks your heart when you look at the world?

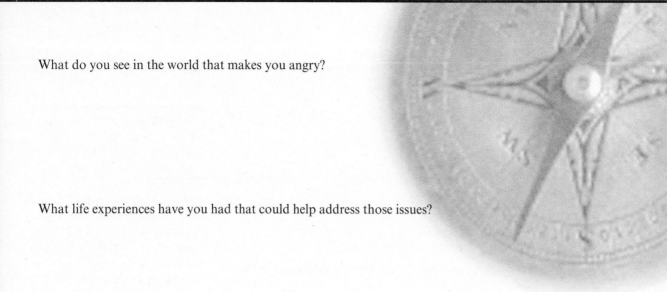

What do you see in the world that makes you angry?

What life experiences have you had that could help address those issues?

What could be your next step toward growth in the practice of service?

As a way of summarizing your reflections for the week, turn now to the Appendix and complete the Gifts-based Service Profile (page 111).

Prayer

O God, the needs are so great. It is overwhelming and heartbreaking. We do not know or fully understand all of your plans, but we want to know your will. Help me to respond to the broken places in the world that you have prepared me to address through the use of my gifts. Give me the willingness to search the unique passion that you scripted in me. Reveal that passion to me, and help me to discover the ministry that will grow me in faith and unity with you so that I might share your love with others. In Jesus' name I pray. Amen.

Week 6: Witness
Invitational Evangelism

What comes to your mind when you hear the word *evangelism*?

For many people, the term *evangelism* has a bad reputation because of the way it has been abused by mean-spirited preachers and manipulative politicians. Others are intimidated by the idea of sharing their faith. Some suggest that faith in Christ is a private affair, not to be shared with others.

In spite of our hesitations, the New Testament is clear that we are called to share the good news of what God has done in Christ with others. Jesus' last command was to go into all the world and make disciples of all people (see Matthew 28:19). In our United Methodist membership vows we promise to participate in the mission of the church through our *witness*.[1]

As United Methodists, we share the gospel without cramming religious truisms down people's throats, hitting people over the head with contrived clichés, or shouting condemnations from the street corners. We share the gospel in the spirit of love and grace at the center of our Wesleyan tradition. While there are many ways in which we bear witness to our faith through word and deed, this week we will focus on what it means to share your witness through *invitational evangelism*.

Rising to sing my Savior's praise,
Thee may I publish all day long;
And let Thy precious word of grace
Flow from my heart, and fill my tongue,
Fill all my life with purest love,
And join me to the Church above.

—*Charles Wesley*[2]

WEEK 6: DAY 1
WHAT IS THE GOOD NEWS?

Scripture Reading
Read the following:
    Romans 5:1-11
    Acts 3:11-26

Today's Message

Have you heard any *good* news lately?

The word *gospel* means "good news." So, what is the good news that Jesus' disciples have to share?

Imagine you are having lunch with a colleague and he or she initiates a conversation about faith. Imagine that he or she has questions about your involvement in your congregation or your relationship with Christ and then directly asks you to explain what it means for you to be a Christian. How would you respond? Write your response below:

John Wesley centered the Methodist movement in three essential beliefs:

1) original sin
2) justification by faith alone
3) holiness of heart and life[3]

Original sin: In Genesis, we discover that we are made in the image of God, but our image is fractured by sin and needs to be restored. Romans 3:23 tells us that all humans sin and fall short of the glory of God. Being a "good person" is not enough to reconcile us to God and heal the brokenness of our world.

Justification by faith: Our image is restored and we are justified—made right with God—when we come to faith in Christ. Justification means that God's love fully revealed in Christ brings us into right relationship with God and with one another. All that is needed is for us to acknowledge our need, receive God's love and grace as a gift, and align our living with God's love.

Holiness of heart and life: God's work in our lives is not finished when we profess faith in Christ. The Holy Spirit continues to be at work in us to form us into the likeness of Christ. Wesley called this work of grace "sanctification." The Holy Spirit in us leads toward "holiness"—the wholeness of a life that is fully centered in loving God and loving others.

Because Christianity in the western part of the world tends to focus on privatized spiritual experiences, it is important to highlight that the restoration that Jesus provides addresses not only individual sin but also systemic sin. The ultimate purpose of Jesus' life, death, and resurrection is not only reconciliation of individuals to God but also the reconciliation of "all things in him, things in heaven and things on earth" (Ephesians 1:10). God's love in Christ connects Christians to a common mission to redeem the world and restore all of humanity to the loving, saving, life-giving purpose of God that Jesus called the kingdom of God. The invitation to each of us is to recognize our deep need for realignment, receive the grace that only God can give, and join with the church in participating in God's transformation of the world.

That's the big story of the good news. But the good news becomes personal when it becomes *our* story, the story of the way the love of God has touched, healed, and transformed our lives. The New Testament book of Acts describes the way the good news spread as ordinary people shared their own stories of the way Christ had touched their lives.

You may be comfortable sharing your story, or you may believe that your story isn't dramatic enough to share it with others. Wherever you are, God doesn't intend for you to stay there. God can and will use your story if you are ready to share it.

Choose one of the passages from today's Scripture Reading and use SOAPY or *Lectio Divina* (see pages 45-47). Record your notes of the experience below:

> O that the world might know
> the all-atoning Lamb!
> Spirit of faith, descend and
> show the virtue of his name;
> the grace which all may find,
> the saving power, impart,
> and testify to humankind,
> and speak in every heart.
> —Charles Wesley[4]

Your Reflections
How have you experienced the transformative power of God's love?

How have you felt the impact of God's free gift of love and grace in your life?

On a scale of one to ten, with one being very uncomfortable and ten being very comfortable, how comfortable are you with sharing the good news? Circle your answer.

1   2   3   4   5   6   7   8   9   10

If you can't articulate what the good news is, what are your questions about it?

What steps do you need to take to improve your comfort level in sharing the good news?

How have God's love and grace made a difference in your life?

Prayer

God, thank you for the undeserved gift of your love. Help me grow in my ability to share the good news of Jesus Christ in both word and deed. Amen.

Week 6: Day 2
Who Was Your Andrew or Philip?

Scripture Reading
Read the following:
   John 1:35-51

Use SOAPY or *Lectio Divina* (see pages 45-47) to explore John 1:35-51. Record notes of your experience below:

Today's Message
There's an odd thing about the Gospel according to John. The first time we hear Jesus speak, he is not teaching, preaching, or praying; he is asking a question. It could, in fact, be the question the Gospel writer wants to ask all of us: "When Jesus turned and saw them following, he said to them, 'What are you looking for?'" (John 1:38).

So, what are we *really* looking for?

What is the nagging hunger in the human soul for something that cannot be purchased at the mall on Saturday afternoon?

What is the deep longing that tugs at our hearts when we are alone in the darkness of the night?

What are we looking for even before we know that we are looking for it?

John's answer is *life*. But it's not just any kind of life.

It's a special kind of life called "eternal life."

Life that is not bounded by the finite categories of time and space.

Life that is fully alive with the life of God.

Life that is not something we wait to experience until we get to heaven, but a way of living that begins right here and now.

Life that Jesus defined as loving God with our whole hearts, souls, minds, and strength and loving others the way we have been loved by God.

Eternal life. That's what these followers of John the Baptist were looking for when they started following Jesus. Jesus' invitation to them was, "Come and see" (John 1:39). They spent the remainder of the day with Jesus. Then Andrew immediately went to find his brother Simon. He told his brother, "We have found the Messiah" (John 1:41). They had found the "anointed one," the one who is God's life present in human life. Andrew brought Simon to Jesus. Jesus recognized Simon as if he had known him for a long time and renamed him Peter.

It happened again the next day when Jesus found Philip and Philip immediately went to find Nathanael. He told Nathanael, "We have found him" (John 1:45). Philip offered Nathanael the same invitation Jesus had offered to him: "Come and see."

Were it not for Andrew and Philip being willing to share their stories, Peter and Nathanael never would have followed Jesus and seen their lives transformed. After experiencing eternal life in Jesus for themselves, they shared their stories with someone else. But notice that they didn't begin by telling their stories to total strangers. They began with people they knew—people who knew them.

We see the same process at work in the story of the woman Jesus met at the Samaritan well (John 4:1-42). After meeting Jesus, she ran to all of her neighbors and said, "Come and see a man who told me everything I have ever done!" (John 4:29). They came and saw, with the result that "many Samaritans from that city believed in him because of the woman's testimony" (John 4:39).

Now, that's *invitational evangelism* at its best! It's one person sharing with another person how he or she has experienced God's love in Christ and offering the invitation, "Come and see."

Your Reflections

Who has been like Andrew and Philip in your life? Write the names of the people in your past who shared their faith with you.

How did they communicate their faith? What did they say? What did they do?

How did it make you feel? What kind of impression did it make? What about it connected with you?

When has someone shared his or her faith with you less than effectively? What about the person's witness did not connect?

Prayer

God, thank you for the people in my past who introduced me to Jesus. Help me find those within my own life with whom I can share my story and offer the invitation, "Come and see." Amen.

Week 6: Day 3
Your Story Is Important!

Scripture Reading

Read the following:

Romans 10:13-17

1 John 1:1-4

Today's Message

Consider this: the church has been around for two thousand years, touching every generation of humanity since Christ and spanning every continent on earth. Countless numbers of people have come to know and experience the saving love of Christ and have had their lives transformed. The witness of the church has resulted in seismic changes in the culture, from the abolition of slavery in England and America to the struggle against apartheid in South Africa; from giving women the right to vote to feeding starving people. How has this happened? It has happened one life at a time. It is the result of individual lives being transformed and those lives being bound together in the body of Christ. It happens when people allow the story of the gospel to become the story by which they live, from one generation to another. It happens when followers of Jesus begin applying the values of the kingdom of God to the critical issues of the world around them.

One day a boy asked his mother, "Remember that antique vase that has been passed down from generation to generation in our family?" She replied, "Yes, what about it?" The boy confessed, "This generation just dropped it."

We can't be the generation to drop the vase! Jesus' love must continue to be shared in word and deed. It can be made real only as people like you share your story and become the living expression of God's love in the lives of others. The gospel is passed on by our witness.

Sharing our stories is a vital component of our spiritual development as followers of Jesus and becomes part of the fulfillment of the church's mission. When a person is open to hearing your story, all he or she usually wants to know is this:

- what you were like before you experienced Christ
- how you came to know and experience him
- what you've been like after surrendering your life to him

Witnessing is about building relationships and sharing our stories of what God has done for us in a genuine and natural way. It's often been said that sharing Christ is like one beggar telling another beggar where to find bread.

You may be thinking, *No way!* Maybe you don't feel that you have much of a story to tell. Yours may not seem very dramatic, compelling, or special. Maybe you don't feel that religion is something that ought to be brought up in conversation. It's too private, too personal, and too individual. Maybe you have too much baggage associated with previous church experiences that have warped the meaning of the *e* word—*evangelism*.

Your anxieties are real, but the solution is much simpler than you think. Evangelism is sharing your story in whatever way God has uniquely wired you to do so. It's about doing the work of Christ and being his witness in the way you live your life. Regardless of how you do it, the important thing is *that* you do it. In the end, that's all Jesus calls each of us to do.

Believe it or not, your story is important. It includes joy, sorrow, pain, faith, and love. You know it better than anyone else, and it is important to God. God wants to use it to continue God's greatest ongoing project: the transformation of the world! It will make an eternal difference.

Your Reflections

What were you like prior to experiencing Christ? If you came to faith at a young age, how has it shaped the way you have lived?

How did you come to know and experience Christ?
Describe the circumstances that moved you to accept God's grace.
If possible, identify the most significant thing or things that God used to initiate your decision.

What have you been like after surrendering your life to Christ?

"Good evangelists . . . are people who engage others in good conversation about important and profound topics. . . . They do this, not because they like to be experts and impose their views on others, but because they feel they are in fact sent by God to do so. They live with a sense of mission that their God-given calling in life is not just to live selfishly, or even just to live well, but to in fact live unselfishly and well *and* to help others live unselfishly and well too."
—Brian D. McLaren[6]

Prayer
Teach me, Lord, to share my witness with others. I want to be part of something that's bigger than my self-interest. I want to live unselfishly and well and to invite others to live that way too. In Jesus' name. Amen.

WEEK 6: DAY 4
HOW WILL I SHARE MY STORY?

Scripture Reading
Read the following:
- 2 Corinthians 10:1-5
- 2 Timothy 4:1-5
- Matthew 5:14-16

Today's Message

We are all called to share our witness in word and in deed. But everyone is not called to share his or her witness in exactly the same way. We have different personalities, different relational styles, and different perspectives on life. These differences are critical when it comes to sharing the love of Christ with others. Think about it. Not everyone needs to hear about Jesus in exactly the same way. There is no universal formula, no standard script, no perfect equation for being a witness. Instead, God has given you your way. Even as the word of God became incarnate in the life of Jesus, so the living Word can become incarnate through your life.

The comical story is told of the man who fell into a well. While waiting and praying for someone to come and save him, he experienced God's grace and made a commitment to Christ. He was so passionate about helping other people find what he had found that he spent the rest of his life pushing other people into wells.

The story points to the difference between the reality of God's love and the constantly changing circumstances in which people experience it. We share our stories not to make other people experience Christ in exactly the same way that we did, but to bear witness to the reality behind the experience.

Being a witness for Christ is similar to being a witness in a courtroom. The witness is not called to argue the case. That job belongs to the attorney. The witness is not called to issue a verdict. That job belongs to the jury. The witness is not called to rule on the case. That job belongs to the judge. Witnesses are simply called to describe their own experience—what they saw, heard, or observed. At its core, being a witness for Christ simply means sharing with someone else what we have experienced in Jesus Christ.

The form that our witness takes will be uniquely fitted to who we are. In his book *Building a Contagious Church,* Mark Mittelberg presents six styles of sharing Christ with other people: intellectual, confrontational, testimonial, interpersonal, invitational, and serving.[7] Among these six styles, there is likely to be at least one style that fits you best. As you reflect on the Scriptures associated with them, circle the style that fits you.

Intellectual
We demolish arguments and every pretension that sets itself up against the knowledge of God, and we take captive every thought to make it obedient to Christ. (2 Corinthians 10:5 NIV)

Confrontational
Proclaim the message; be persistent whether the time is favorable or unfavorable; convince, rebuke, and encourage, with the utmost patience in teaching. (2 Timothy 4:2)

Testimonial
We declare to you what we have seen and heard so that you also may have fellowship with us; and truly our fellowship is with the Father and with his Son Jesus Christ. (1 John 1:3)

Interpersonal

To the weak I became weak, so that I might win the weak. I have become all things to all people, that I might by all means save some. (1 Corinthians 9:22)

Invitational

Then the master said to the slave, "Go out into the roads and lanes, and compel people to come in, so that my house may be filled." (Luke 14:23)

Serving

Let your light shine before others, so that they may see your good works and give glory to your Father in heaven. (Matthew 5:16)

Which form of witness is right for you? The good news is that the spirit of God can be at work through the unique witness of your life. Even better, you are not in this alone. The spirit of God can take the unique experiences of your life and use them to bear witness to the transforming love and grace of God.

> "I have one point in view to promote, so far as I am able, vital, practical religion; and by the grace of God to beget, preserve, and increase the life of God in the souls of men."
>
> —John Wesley[8]

Your Reflections

Review "Your Reflections" for Day 3 of this week. Combining and building upon your responses, use the following page to write your story of coming to be a follower of Jesus in 100-200 words. Tell what your life was like before Christ, how you came to be a follower of Christ, and what your life has been like since. Keep these four guidelines in mind:

1) Keep it short.
2) Keep it clear.
3) Make it simple (avoid "religion-ese").
4) Make it accessible.

Prayer

God, thank you for making me a unique person who is gifted in a special way to reach out to particular people. In Jesus' name. Amen.

My Story:

WEEK 6: DAY 5
DO I HAVE A WITNESS?

Scripture Reading
Read the following:
    Matthew 28:16-20
    Acts 1:1-8

Today's Message

In African American churches, it is not unusual for the preacher to call out to the congregation, "Do I have a witness?" It's a way of testing the truth of the gospel in personal experience. It could also be the question the risen Christ is constantly asking of his disciples.

In his farewell message to his disciples, Jesus promised that by the power of the Holy Spirit, they would be his witnesses (Acts 1:8). No one was more surprised than those disciples when it actually happened (Acts 2:1-11)! According to the book of Acts, the church grew not by slick marketing campaigns or highly organized programs, but by followers of Jesus sharing the story of what God had done and doing what Jesus would have them do.

The story of the spiritual awakening that accompanied the consecration of the new cathedral in Coventry, England, is like something straight out of the book of Acts. Stephen Verney told the story in his book *Fire in Coventry*. He named three lessons they learned about "The New Evangelism," which we have adapted here:[9]

1. "We have got to be the thing we proclaim." We are called to live together in a community in which others may see the forgiveness, love, compassion, and joy of Jesus. The viability of our witness is directly related to the integrity of our life together.
2. Evangelism is "the inevitable outpouring of love." Verney said that "if the fire of love is burning in a church that church cannot help evangelizing, and if the fire is not burning, then all its evangelistic effort is . . . useless." When we fail to reach out to others, it is a sign of the lack of spiritual vitality in our lives.
3. "There is a *method* of evangelism." Both individuals and congregations need to think through the processes by which we share the good news and invite others to "come and see." It involves looking at our church from the outside in, rather than from the inside out. It means understanding the needs of the people around us and intentionally choosing the method of witness that is most appropriate for them.

Can you hear Jesus saying, "Do I have a witness?" Will you be the person who answers, "Yes"?

Your Reflections

How comfortable are you in sharing your story? What can you do to become more comfortable?

How often do you find ways to share your faith with others (with words and actions)?

Do you know people for whom you can be praying and who need to hear about Jesus *from you*? Identify three:

Pray that the Spirit guides you in knowing how to share your faith with these individuals. Spend some time right now praying for the individuals you have listed, and be alert to opportunities for sharing Christ with them. Record your thoughts below:

What could be your next step toward growth in the practice of invitational evangelism?

What about your local congregation? How contagious is the spirit of evangelism and hospitality within it? What would people experience if they responded to an invitation to "come and see"?

> "We must remember that methods, even at their best, are *after the fact.* We need a passion, a sublime focus. Such a passion will not take the place of methods; but our methods will never be anything more than idle machinery unless we have an impulse that will make us rise up and march, reach out and love, kneel down and pray."
> —J. Ellsworth Kalas[10]

Prayer

My gracious Master and my God,
assist me to proclaim,
to spread through all the earth abroad
the honors of thy name.
                    —Charles Wesley[11]

A Final Day
A Time for Commitment

Scripture Reading

Read the following and use SOAPY or *Lectio Divina* (see pages 45-47):

    1 Timothy 4:8-16

    Luke 9:23-27

Record your notes of the experience below:

Today's Message

You are being invited to make a commitment to follow Christ and participate in the global body of Christ through a local United Methodist faith community. This class is intended to help you live out that commitment to Christ. Today you have reached the time to make decisions about what your next steps will be in the individual practices of the following:

- Prayer and Scripture meditation (prayers): Your commitment to daily prayer, Bible reflection, and the discipleship journey.
- Corporate worship and small-group community (presence): The number of Sundays you will be in corporate worship during the year, and where you plan to be involved in small-group life to grow your faith.

- Financial generosity (gifts): Your financial commitment to the ministry of the church.
- Spiritual gifts and gifts-based service (service): Where you will serve in the body of Christ.
- Invitational evangelism (witness): How you will share your faith story with others.

Throughout *A Disciple's Path*, you have reflected on where God is calling you in these areas. Say a prayer and fill out the Commitment Card or form provided by your leader. *Remember, only commit to what God is calling you to do.* Don't do anything out of guilt, but do feel challenged to take the next step. Only fill out what you are ready to commit to, not what you are interested in. Bring the card with you to group session 6.

These spiritual disciplines are the practices by which we grow into disciples of Jesus who love God with our whole hearts, souls, minds, and strength and who love others the way we have been loved by God. They are the tangible expression of our commitment to share in the ministry of the church and become a part of God's transformation of the world. You are a vital part of this mission!

As you make your prayerful decisions, know that there will be obstacles in the road, things that will attempt to prevent you from following through on the commitments you will make. But know that your fellow disciples walk this pathway with you. You are not alone.

Spiritual maturity takes time, discipline, and devotion. Spiritual apathy or indifference can sneak in. If we are not growing—if we are stagnant in our faith— it usually leads to backsliding. But hang in there! The journey is more than worth the effort because it is the way that leads to vibrant, joyful, eternal life!

106

Your Reflections

How disciplined have I been during this course?

What has been difficult for me, and how can I invite God into the difficulty?

What is the most significant learning that I will take with me from this experience?

What difference has this experience made in the way I intend
to live my life as a disciple of Jesus Christ?

Prayer

A charge to keep I have,
a God to glorify,
a never-dying soul to save,
and fit it for the sky.
To serve the present age,
my calling to fulfill;
O may it all my powers engage
to do my Master's will!
Arm me with jealous care,
as in thy sight to live,
and oh, thy servant, Lord,
prepare
a strict account to give!
Help me to watch and pray,
and on thyself rely,
assured, if I my trust betray,
I shall forever die.
                        —Charles Wesley[12]

APPENDIX

Small-group Community Profile

List small groups in which you have been involved in the past:

In what ways has your small-group involvement contributed to your spiritual growth?

List small groups in which you currently are involved:

In what ways do these groups assist you in growing your faith?

List small groups in which you would like to participate:

What could be your next step toward growth in the practice of small-group community?

How would you explain or describe the importance of Christian community?

Gifts-based Service Profile

Have you taken the online spiritual gifts assessment?   **Yes / No**

If not, please take the assessment at http://survey.adultbiblestudies.com/ before continuing.

What was surprising or challenging to you in the results?

List your three top spiritual gifts (in order):

(1)_____ (2) _____ (3) _____

What skills/talents would you like to employ in ministry (education, employment, hobbies, interests, abilities)?

What is your "holy discontent"? What do you see in the world that breaks your heart?

Are you currently using your gifts serving in the church?   **Yes / No**
 If yes, where?

Are you currently using your gifts serving outside the church?   **Yes / No**
 If yes, where?

What questions do you have about using your spiritual gifts in building up the body of Christ?

In what areas of ministry would you like to use your gifts in serving the church?

Selecting a Bible

When selecting a Bible for your own use, there are three main considerations:

1) translation or version
2) study helps and special features
3) special editions

1) Translation or Version

When scholars begin a new translation, they tend to follow one of three basic translation methods:

1) Formal equivalent – Keeps as close as possible to the phrasing (syntax) in the original language. These translations often sound awkward but are best used for academic study, especially when learning Hebrew and Greek.

2) Dynamic equivalent – Translates words, grammatical construction, and idioms into accurate English expressions. Dynamic translations are particularly suited for general reading, prayer, and devotional study.

3) Paraphrase – Paraphrases the ideas into more colloquial English, often with additional interpretation embedded into the sentences.

Overview of Popular Translations

New Revised Standard Version (NRSV)
Published in 1989, based on the Revised Standard Version (RSV) of 1952. Dignified, formal language in the tradition of the King James Version. Uses gender-inclusive language in references to human beings. Some editions include the Apocrypha.

Common English Bible (CEB)
Published in 2011. Smooth reading in plain English. Outstanding balance between accuracy and readability. One hundred and twenty translators from twenty-four denominations included women for the first time in Bible translation teams. Oral field testing among congregations in thirteen denominations makes the CEB especially suitable for worship use and devotional study. Some editions for Anglicans and Catholics include the Apocrypha.

New International Version (NIV)
Published in 1984, revised modestly in 2010 by partial use of gender inclusive language. Clear and dignified reading in English. Good balance between accuracy and readability. Heavily influenced among the translators by Reformed interpretation.

King James Version (KJV)
Published in 1611, based on the earlier work of William Tyndale, and authorized by King James of England. First widely available English translation of the Bible. Competed with the Geneva Bible for two centuries in America but prevailed until the 1980s as the dominant English translation. Though still available and used by more than 25 percent of Bible readers, this version's Elizabethan language makes reading difficult for many readers.

New King James Version (NKJV)
Published in 1982, updating the original King James Version. Easier word usage, removed thee and thou, but somewhat choppy because it maintains seventeenth-century sentence structure. Intended to update and modernize while preserving as much as possible of the original.

New American Bible (NAB)
Published in 2011 and updated significantly from the 1970 edition; authorized by bishops from the Roman Catholic Church. A more formal translation in 2011. Includes Apocrypha in all editions.

New American Standard Bible (NASB)
Published in 1971 and updated modestly in 1995. Formal and awkward style but more readable than the King James Version.

Amplified (AMP)
Published in 1964 and updated in 1987. Formal translation plus additional paraphrase of word meanings by means of a system of brackets and parentheses. A popular translation for understanding hidden meanings of Greek and Hebrew words.

The New Living Translation (NLT)
Published in 1996, replacing The Living Bible (TLB) by Ken Taylor of 1971, which was a very popular paraphrase of the Bible. The NLT changed to a dynamic equivalent translation while retaining some tendency to paraphrase.

The Message
Published in 2002. An easy-to-read, colloquial paraphrase by Eugene Petersen. Develops the tone and rhythms of American English speech with creative emphasis on contemporary idioms.

2) Study Helps and Special Features

Most translations can be found with or without study helps and other special features. Many readers find the study helps in a "study Bible" indispensable and worth the extra cost. Nearly all study helps include such things as maps, cross-references, and a concordance. The key difference between most study Bibles is the nature of the explanatory notes, which fall into three major categories:

1) Bible Knowledge Study Notes
These include historical overviews, theological discussions, book introductions, and verse-by-verse commentary. Often these notes are based on the commentator's theological beliefs; in this case, comparison between more than one study Bible is suggested.

2) Devotional Study Notes

These notes, which may be incorporated with any of the different translations of the Bible, include daily meditations and often are published in Bibles with a specific theme, such as a new believer Bible, a woman's or man's Bible, a teen Bible, and so forth.

3) Life Application Study Notes

These notes also are aimed at a particular audience, such as women or students, and focus on solutions to life's problems (such as relationships or money or culture).

Study helps and special features also may include the following:

Cross References: A listing of other Scriptures that pertain to the same subject or quote the same material.

Concordance: An index of key words in the Bible and the Scriptures where they are found. Very helpful for finding a verse when you know only key words. Remember that concordances are generally keyed to a particular translation.

Timelines: Since the books of the Bible are not in chronological order, timelines help give valuable perspective on the relationship between biblical and historical events.

Topical Index: A listing of Bible verses that deal with a particular subject. Where a concordance would show you Scriptures that contain the word "love," a topical index would list Scriptures about "love."

Biographies: Many Bibles contain brief biographical material about persons in the Bible—information about their contributions, character, family, and so forth.

Bible Book Outline and Introduction: Insightful information about each book of the Bible including key events, main characters, its author, and main points.

Gospel Parallels or Gospel Harmony: The four Gospels—Matthew, Mark, Luke, and John—cover much of the same material, but each has a different author and perspective. Each of the books contains some unique material as well. A Gospel Parallel presents a line for line comparison of these four books. A Gospel Harmony combines the four stories into a hypothetical single story. The parallel is preferred because a harmony glosses over important chronological distinctions and makes decisions that reduce the distinctive theology of each story about Jesus.

3) Special Editions

Many special edition Bibles are available for a wide variety of uses. You might like to choose a special edition Bible that seems to be designed just for you, or it may be that you receive one as a gift. Examples of special edition Bibles include the following:

Children's Bibles
Youth Bibles
Student Bibles

Women's Bibles
Men's Bibles
Reference Bibles
Parallel Bibles (include more than one translation)
Devotional Bibles
Life Application Bibles
Gift and Award Bibles
Large or Giant Print Bibles
Outreach Bibles

Additional Resources

Many additional resources are available in print and online to help you read and understand the Scriptures, such as commentaries, Bible dictionaries, Bible encyclopedias, and Bible handbooks. There also are many books, devotions, and study guides available to help you study individual books of the Bible, Bible history, and key people in the Bible.

Online Resources
http://www.cokesbury.com
http://commonenglishbible.com
http://www.crosswalk.com/
http://www.biblegateway.com/
http://www.blueletterbible.org

SPIRITUAL GIFTS OVERVIEW

The spiritual gifts appear in bold. Each gift's contribution to the church is printed in italics below the gift. Descriptive words that often characterize persons with that particular gift are listed below the gift and its contribution.

Administration
Efficiency

Conscientious
Objective
Efficient
Organized
Responsible
Thorough
Goal-oriented

Apostleship
New Ministries

Entrepreneurial
Cause-driven
Risk-taking
Adaptable
Adventurous
Culturally Sensitive

Distinguishing of Spirits
Clarity

Insightful
Truthful
Challenging
Intuitive
Sensitive
Perceptive
Decisive

Encouragement
Strength and Comfort

Affirming
Motivating
Consoling
Challenging
Reassuring
Comforting
Positive

Evangelism
The Good News
Confident
Relational
Faith Sharing
Outgoing
Spiritual
Challenging
Communicator

Faith
Confidence
Prayerful
Assured
Trusting
Inspiring
Optimistic
Positive
Hopeful

Giving
Resources
Charitable
Generous
Responsible
Disciplined
Trusts in God
Good Steward
Resourceful

Healing
Wholeness
Compassionate
Trusts in God
Faith-filled
Powerful in Prayer
Humble
Spiritual
Submissive

Helps (Serving)
Assistance
Available
Reliable
Practical
Dependable
Willing
Selfless
Servant-oriented

Hospitality
Food and Fellowship
Friendly
Gracious
Inviting
Trusting
Caring
Responsible
Warm

Leadership
Direction
Diligent
Visionary
Persuasive
Influential
Role Model
Motivating
Inspiring

Mercy
Care
Empathetic
Compassionate
Sensitive
Responsible
Kind
Caring
Burden-bearing

Message of Knowledge
Awareness
Inquisitive
Responsive
Observant
Insightful
Reflective
Studious
Truthful

Message of Wisdom
Guidance
Reasonable
Thoughtful
Insightful
Skillful
Sensible

Pastor-Teacher
Shepherding
Influencing
Nurturing
Guiding
Disciple-maker
Protective

Prophecy
Conviction
Confronting
Penetrating
Compelling
Outspoken
Uncompromising
Authentic

Teaching
Application
Articulate
Analytical
Practical
Studious
Authoritative

Some of these ministry areas are the responsibility only of those gifted to fulfill them, while others are the responsibility of all believers. For instance, those with the gift of prophecy should preach; those with the gift of teaching should teach the Bible to others; those with the gift of apostleship should be our leaders in missions. On the other hand, God expects all of us to discern truth from error, share our faith, encourage others, have faith in God, give sacrificially, show hospitality to others, intercede regularly, seek to know and share God's word, offer mercy to hurting people, meet practical needs with joy, help others grow spiritually, and relate God's truth to life.

Whether we are gifted in these areas or not, we are responsible to meet these needs as God directs us. Those with spiritual gifts in these areas typically will be called to lead the rest of us in these ministries and will model them with great effectiveness. Those who possess the gift of evangelism encourage the rest of us to share our faith when they demonstrate their gift in action. Those with the gift of serving take the initiative to help in this area and show the rest of us how to serve with joy.

The spiritual gifts do not confine our service only to the areas where we are gifted. Rather, they point the way to ministries where we will lead and serve with our greatest passion and joy.

A Note About the Charismatic Gifts

Not listed on the chart are three gifts that are often called "charismatic" gifts of the Spirit that point to God and/or are signs of God's power: speaking in tongues, interpretation of tongues, and miraculous powers. John Wesley categorized these as the "extraordinary gifts" of the Spirit in contrast to the "ordinary graces of the gospel."[1] The Apostle Paul acknowledged the way these gifts can be manipulated or abused by carefully defining the boundaries around them, always pointing to "the greatest gift" of love (1 Corinthians 13).

The use of the "extraordinary gifts" has not generally been at the center of Methodist belief or practice. Most United Methodists see the gift of "tongues" from the perspective of the Pentecost story (Acts 2), in which the Holy Spirit enabled each person to hear the good news in the context of his or her own language and culture. Rather than be concerned about esoteric expressions of the "extraordinary gifts," we see them expressed in the "ordinary" ways in which we share our life in Christ in the rich diversity of culture, language, and tradition in the body of Christ. With the Corinthian Christians, we are always called to the way of love.

SPIRITUAL GIFTS DESCRIPTIONS

The following descriptions are adapted from *Serving from the Heart: Finding Your Gifts and Talents for Service* by Carol Cartmill and Yvonne Gentile (Abingdon Press, 2011).

Administration – Organizing people and ministries efficiently.
This is the God-given ability to organize and manage information, people, events, and resources to accomplish the objectives of a ministry. People with this gift handle details carefully and thoroughly. They are skilled in determining priorities and in planning and directing the steps needed to achieve a goal. They often make it easier for others to use their own gifts simply by keeping things organized and flowing smoothly.

Apostleship – Adapting to a different culture to share the gospel or do ministry.
This gift is the divine ability to build the foundation of new churches by preaching the word, teaching others to live by Christ's commandments through the example of their own lives, and preparing the people to serve one another. Persons with this gift are not only eager to bring the gospel to those who have never heard it; they prepare those people to continue the work after they have left. They enthusiastically approach new ministries, churches, or settings and realize the need to adapt methods of evangelism and service to widely different environments.

Distinguishing of Spirits – Recognizing what is of God and what is not of God.
This gift is the divine ability to distinguish between good and evil, truth and error, and pure motives and impure motives. People with this gift usually can rely on instincts or first impressions to tell when a person or message is deceptive or inconsistent with biblical truths. They can sense the presence of evil, and they question motives, intentions, doctrine, deeds, and beliefs. These people must take care to use their gift in a way that brings good to the body of Christ—to judge with mercy and understanding rather than to condemn.

Encouragement – Encouraging others to grow in their faith.
This is the God-given ability to encourage, help, intercede for, and be an advocate for others in a way that motivates them to grow in their faith and urges them to action. This gift takes many forms and can be done through personal relationships, music, writings, intercessory prayer, and speaking, to name a few. People with this gift encourage others to remain faithful even in the midst of struggles. They are sensitive and sympathetic toward another person's emotional state and exhort selflessly, with affection, not contempt. They can see positive traits or aspects that other persons overlook and often have more faith in other persons than they have in themselves.

Evangelism – Sharing the gospel with others.
This is the divine ability to spread the good news of Jesus Christ so that unknowing persons respond with faith and discipleship. People with this gift speak simply and comfortably about their faith, and nonbelievers are drawn into this circle of comfort. These people enjoy many friendships outside of their Christian community. They enjoy helping others see how Christianity can fulfill their needs. They eagerly study questions that challenge Christianity and respond clearly in ways that connect with individuals, meeting them right where they are.

Faith – Seeing God's plan and following it with confidence.
This is the divine ability to recognize what God wants done and to act when others fall back in doubt. Although as Christians we all are called to have faith, people with this gift receive it in an extraordinary measure. Even in the face of barriers that overwhelm others, people with this gift simply have confidence that God will see God's will done. Believing deeply in the power of prayer, they also know that God is both present and active in their lives. People with this gift show others by their works and their words that God is faithful to God's promises.

Giving – Sharing resources freely and joyfully.
This is the God-given ability to give generously of material wealth, knowing that spiritual wealth will abound as God's work is advanced. Those with this gift are not always affluent but are always generous with what they do have. They usually manage their finances well, may have a special ability to make money, and tend to be frugal in their lifestyle. They use these skills to increase their support for God's work, trusting that God will provide for their needs. They are often comfortable and successful in approaching others for gifts. Instead of asking, "How much of my money do I give to God?" they ask, "How much of God's money do I keep?"

Healing – Bringing wholeness to others.
This gift is the divine ability to bring physical, emotional, or spiritual wholeness to others. People with this gift listen skillfully as they seek God's guidance to learn the needs of the sick and to determine the causes and nature of an illness. They believe that God can cure and that prayer can overcome any negative forces at work (but they also recognize that God might have a different plan). Their tools include prayer, touch, and spoken words. This gift shows God's power; at the same time, it is to God's glory. The goal of healing is not just healing itself, but spreading the gospel by pointing to the power of Jesus Christ and to show the glory of God.

Helps (Serving) – Providing aid and relief with which to meet practical needs.
This gift is the God-given ability to work alongside others in performing practical and often behind-the-scene tasks to sustain and enhance the body of Christ. People with this gift receive spiritual satisfaction from doing everyday necessary tasks; they may prefer to work quietly and without public recognition. When they see a need, they frequently take care of it without being asked. Their work often frees up other persons so that they may carry out their own ministries.

Hospitality – Making others feel welcome and comfortable.
This is the divine ability to make others feel safe, accepted, and comfortable. People with this gift often love to entertain. Sometimes, however, their gift is simply demonstrated by a warm handshake or hug, a bright smile, and a tendency to greet new people and help them get acclimated to a new place or situation. People are drawn to persons with this gift—they often have many acquaintances or friends and help others make connections, too.

Leadership – Motivating and inspiring others.
This is the divine ability to motivate, coordinate, and direct people doing God's work. People with this gift are visionaries who inspire others to work together to make the vision a reality. They take responsibility for setting and achieving goals. They step in where there is a lack of direction. They build a team of talented persons and then empower them. These persons are called to be servant-leaders. Held to a high moral standard, they lead by the example of their own lives.

Mercy – Ministering to others with compassion.

This is the God-given ability to see and feel the suffering of others and to minister to them with love and understanding. More simply, this gift is "compassion in action." People with this gift are called to reach out to someone who is hurt or rejected, easing his or her suffering. They feel fulfilled when they can show others that God loves them. They are skilled at gaining the trust of those in need and enjoy finding ways to comfort them.

Message of Knowledge – Discerning and sharing God's purposes.

This is the God-given ability to understand, organize, and effectively use or communicate information to advance God's purposes. The information may come either from the Holy Spirit or from sources around us. People with this gift enjoy studying the Bible and other sources to gain facts, insights, and truths. The term "message of knowledge" is intentional. This gift is not knowledge for one's own benefit—it must be communicated and shared with others. People with this gift use their knowledge for projects, ministries, or teaching. They organize it in order to pass it to others for their use and benefit. The Holy Spirit appears to be at work when these people show unusual insight or understanding.

Message of Wisdom – Relating biblical truth to practical life.

This is the God-given ability to understand and apply biblical and spiritual knowledge to complex, contradictory, or other difficult situations. People with this gift have an ability to understand and live God's will. They share their wisdom with others through teaching and admonition. As with the gift of the Message of Knowledge, the gift of wisdom is not for one's own benefit but must be shared. People with this gift speak God's truth as found in Scripture in order to provide clarity and direction to people who are struggling with which way they should go. They make practical application of biblical truths. They are, in effect, a "compass" for the body of Christ.

Pastor-Teacher – Shepherding others toward spiritual growth.

This is the divine ability to guide, protect, and care for other people as they experience spiritual growth. People with this gift enjoy working with groups of people and nurturing their growth over an extended period of time. Because of these long-term relationships, they establish trust and confidence and are able to take the time to care for the "whole person." They can assess where a person is spiritually and then develop or find places where that person can continue his or her journey of faith. They model compassion. The phrase for this gift in the original Greek indicates one gift—"pastor-teacher," not two gifts, "pastor" and "teacher." The primary difference between a pastor-teacher (or shepherd) and a teacher seems to be the longer-term, holistic care provided (in addition to instruction) by a shepherd, versus a teacher, who may operate in a shorter-term aspect, imparting knowledge and instruction but not necessarily care.

Prophecy – Speaking under inspiration the counsel of God.

This is the God-given ability, out of love for God's people, to proclaim God's truth in a way that makes it relevant to current situations in today's culture and guides others to more faith-informed decisions and actions. The goal is not to condemn but to bring about change or enlightenment. People with this gift listen carefully to God so their words will be God-honoring. They see inconsistencies between people's words/actions and biblical teaching that others overlook or may not catch. Prophets speak to the people, bringing edification, encouragement, and consolation. They warn people of the immediate or future consequences of continuing their current course of action, always ending with a message of hope and restoration if the message is heeded.

Teaching – Imparting the truth through instruction.

This is the divine ability to understand and clearly explain God's truths, as well as to show how we can apply these truths in our lives. People with this gift enjoy studying the Bible and inspire listeners to greater obedience to God's word. They prepare through study and reflection and pay close attention to detail. In addition to communicating facts, they are careful to show that the Scriptures have practical applications. They can adapt their presentation in order to communicate God's message to a particular audience effectively.

Three Charismatic Gifts: Tongues, Interpretation of Tongues, Miracles

These three gifts are often called "charismatic" gifts of the Spirit that point to God and/or are signs of God's power. John Wesley categorized these as the "extraordinary gifts" of the Spirit in contrast to the "ordinary graces of the gospel."[2] The Apostle Paul acknowledged the way these gifts can be manipulated or abused by carefully defining the boundaries around them, always pointing to "the greatest gift" of love (1 Corinthians 13).

The use of the "extraordinary gifts" has not generally been at the center of Methodist belief or practice. Most United Methodists see the gift of "tongues" from the perspective of the Pentecost story (Acts 2), in which the Holy Spirit enabled each person to hear the good news in the context of his or her own language and culture. Rather than be concerned about esoteric expressions of the "extraordinary gifts," we see them expressed in the "ordinary" ways in which we share our life in Christ in the rich diversity of culture, language, and tradition in the body of Christ. With the Corinthian Christians, we are always called to the way of love.

See http://www.umc.org/what-we-believe/spiritual-gifts to learn more about these gifts.

NOTES

Introduction

1. Charles Wesley, "Love Divine, All Loves Excelling," in *The United Methodist Hymnal* (Nashville: The United Methodist Publishing House, 1989), 384.
2. See "The Baptismal Covenant" (I–IV), in *The United Methodist Hymnal* (Nashville: The United Methodist Publishing House, 1989), 38. Also see https://www.umcdiscipleship.org/resources/new-membership-vows-and-ritual-revised-and-corrected (accessed March 21, 2018).
3. "Thoughts Upon Methodism" in *Selections from the Writings of the Rev. John Wesley*, compiled by Herbert Welch (New York: Methodist Book Concern, 1918), 205; appeared in *Arminian Magazine*, 1787.

What Does It Mean to Be a United Methodist?

1. Paraphrased from *The Book of Discipline of The United Methodist Church* (Nashville: The United Methodist Publishing House, 2016), 78-80.

Week 1

1. John H. Sammis, "Trust and Obey," *The United Methodist Hymnal* (Nashville: The United Methodist Publishing House, 1989), 467.
2. John Wesley, Sermon 139, "On Love," http://wesley.nnu.edu/john-wesley/the-sermons-of-john-wesley-1872-edition/sermon-139-on-love/ (accessed August 30, 2017).
3. http://www.tentmaker.org/Quotes/lovequotes.htm (accessed September 20, 2011).
4. Charles Wesley, "Come and Let Us Sweetly Join," http://www.allthelyrics.com/lyrics/charles_wesley/come_and_let_us_sweetly_join-lyrics-1155711.html.
5. "Quotes on God," *Notable Quotes*, http://www.notable-quotes.com/g/god_quotes.html (accessed September 20, 2011).
6. F. Belton Joyner, Jr., *United Methodist Questions, United Methodist Answers* (Louisville: Westminster John Knox Press, 2007), 35-36.
7. See Rueben P. Job, *Three Simple Rules* (Nashville: Abingdon Press, 2007).
8. Charles Wesley, "Come and Let Us Sweetly Join," http://www.allthelyrics.com/lyrics/charles_wesley/come_and_let_us_sweetly_join-lyrics-1155711.html.
9. Carlton C. Buck, "O Lord, May Church and Home Combine," in *The United Methodist Hymnal* (Nashville: The United Methodist Publishing House, 1989), 695.
10. See "The Baptismal Covenant" (I–IV), in *The United Methodist Hymnal* (Nashville: The United Methodist Publishing House, 1989), 38. Also see http://www.umcdiscipleship.org/resources/new-membership-vows-and-ritual-revised-and-corrected (accessed March 21, 2018).
11. John Wesley, letter to John Trembath, *The Works of John Wesley*, Vol. XII (Grand Rapids: Zondervan, 1872 reprint), 254.

Week 2

1. See "The Baptismal Covenant" (I–IV), in *The United Methodist Hymnal* (Nashville: The United Methodist Publishing House, 1989), 38. Also see https://www.umcdiscipleship.org/resources/new-membership-vows-and-ritual-revised-and-corrected (accessed March 21, 2018).
2. Janice Grana, Marjorie Thompson, and Stephen Bryant, *Companions in Christ Participant Book* (Nashville: The Upper Room, 2001), 119.
3. John Wesley, quoted in *The Quotable Mr. Wesley*, ed. W. Stephen Gunter (Atlanta: Candler School of Theology, 1999), 37.
4. http://home.snu.edu/~hculbert/selfexam.htm.
5. Richard Rohr, quoted in Norman Shawchuck and Rueben P. Job, *A Guide to Prayer for All Who Seek God* (Nashville: The Upper Room, 2006), 300.
6. http://en.wikipedia.org/wiki/Homo_unius_libri (accessed September 21, 2011).
7. Diana Hynson, "De-Mystifying the Bible (at Least a Little Bit)," January 2009, for The General Board of Discipleship.
8. Paul Scherer, *The Word God Sent* (New York: Harper & Row, 1965), 33.
9. Donald Thorsen, *The Wesleyan Quadrilateral: Scripture, Tradition, Reason & Experience as a Model of Evangelical Theology* (Lexington, Ky.: Emeth, 2005), 5.
10. *The Book of Discipline of the United Methodist Church* (Nashville: The United Methodist Publishing House, 2016), 82.
11. Ibid., 87.
12. Rueben P. Job, *A Wesleyan Spiritual Reader* (Nashville: Abingdon Press, 1997), 84.
13. The SOAPY explanation and example are adapted from the online journal writings of Dick Wills, which are based on the teaching of Wayne Cordeiro of New Hope Christian Fellowship in Honolulu (www.enewhope.org).
14. Rueben P. Job, *A Wesleyan Spiritual Reader* (Nashville: Abingdon Press, 1997), 15.

Week 3

1. Desmond Tutu, *The Rainbow People of God* (New York: Doubleday, 1994), 125.
2. E. Stanley Jones, *A Song of Ascents* (Nashville: Abingdon Press, 1968), 284.
3. "Preface to 1739 Hymns and Sacred Poems," in *The Works of John Wesley*, Jackson Edition, 14:321.
4. Henri Nouwen, *Letters to Marc about Jesus* (San Francisco: Harper & Row, 1988), 83.
5. Charles Wesley, "Blest Be the Dear Uniting Love," in *The United Methodist Hymnal* (Nashville: The United Methodist Publishing House, 1989), 566.
6. Archbishop William Temple, quoted in *The Oxford Book of Prayer*, ed. George Appleton (Oxford: Oxford University Press, 1985), 3.
7. Liturgy definition, http://en.wikipedia.org/wiki/Liturgy (accessed March 21, 2018).
8. *The Works of John Wesley*, Vol. 14 (Grand Rapids: Zondervan, 1872), 304.
9. Charles Wesley, "Jesus, We Look to Thee," https://hymnary.org/text/jesus_we_look_to_thee (accessed March 21, 2018).
10. *Sacrament* definition, http://en.wikipedia.org/wiki/Anglican_sacraments (accessed September 21, 2011).
11. *Sacro* definition, http://en.wiktionary.org/wiki/sacro#Latin (accessed September 21, 2011).
12. Baptismal Covenant I, in *The United Methodist Hymnal* (Nashville: The United Methodist Publishing House, 1989), 36.
13. Ibid.

14. Ibid., 37.

15. See John Wesley's sermon "The Duty of Constant Communion," http://wesley.nnu.edu/john-wesley/the-sermons-of-john-wesley-1872-edition/sermon-101-the-duty-of-constant-communion/ (accessed March 21, 2018).

16. "This Holy Mystery: A United Methodist Understanding of Holy Communion," https://www.umcdiscipleship.org/resources/this-holy-mystery-a-united-methodist-understanding-of-holy-communion (accessed March 21, 2018).

17. Horatius Bonar, "Here, O My Lord, I See Thee," in *The United Methodist Hymnal*, (Nashville: The United Methodist Publishing House, 1989), 623.

18. http://home.snu.edu/~hculbert/selfexam.htm.

19. Charles Wesley, "All Praise to Our Redeeming Lord," in *The United Methodist Hymnal* (Nashville: The United Methodist Publishing House, 1989), 554.

Week 4

1. John Wesley, "The Use of Money," http://wesley.nnu.edu/john-wesley/-the-sermons-of-john-wesley-1872-edition/sermon-50-the-use-of-money/ (accessed March 21, 2018).

2. Ibid.

3. Gerald W. Keucher, "Put Your Money Where You Want Your Heart to Be," in "Leading Ideas," Lewis Center for Church Leadership, March 18, 2009, http://www.churchleadership.com/leading-ideas/put-your-money-where-you-want-your-heart-to-be/ (accessed March 21, 2018).

4. John Wesley, "The Use of Money," http://wesley.nnu.edu/john-wesley/the-sermons-of-john-wesley-1872-edition/sermon-50-the-use-of-money/ (accessed March 21, 2018).

5. Rueben P. Job, *A Wesleyan Spiritual Reader* (Nashville: Abingdon Press, 1997), 32.

6. William Sloane Coffin, "A Sermon on the Amount," *The Collected Sermons of William Sloane Coffin: The Riverside Years*, Vol. 2 (Louisville: Westminster John Knox, 2008), 195.

7. Rueben P. Job, *A Wesleyan Spiritual Reader* (Nashville: Abingdon Press, 1997), 31.

8. John Wesley, quoted in *The Quotable Mr. Wesley*, ed. W. Stephen Gunter (Atlanta: Candler School of Theology, 1999), 57.

9. John Wesley, "On the Danger of Increasing Riches," http://wesley.nnu.edu/john-wesley/the-sermons-of-john-wesley-1872-edition/sermon-126-on-the-danger-of-increasing-riches/ (accessed March 21, 2018).

Week 5

1. John Ortberg, *The Life You've Always Wanted* (Grand Rapids: Zondervan, 1997), 106.

2. http://www.goodreads.com/quotes/show/74745 (accessed September 29, 2011).

3. *The Book of Discipline of The United Methodist Church* (Nashville: The United Methodist Publishing House, 2016), 97.

4. Stephen Verney, *Fire in Coventry* (Westwood, N.J.: Revell, 1964), 20.

5. Eugene Peterson, *Practice Resurrection* (Grand Rapids: Eerdmans, 2010), 47.

6. Charles Wesley, "Forth in Thy Name, O Lord," in *The United Methodist Hymnal* (Nashville: The United Methodist Publishing House, 1989), 438.

7. http://islandireland.com/Pages/folk/sets/toasts.html (accessed September 24, 2011).

8. Charles Wesley, "Christ, from Whom All Blessings Flow," in *The United Methodist Hymnal* (Nashville: The United Methodist Publishing House, 1989), 550.

9. Paul Wesley Chilcote, *Recapturing the Wesleys' Vision* (Downers Grove, Ill.: InterVarsity, 2004), 101.

Week 6

1. https://www.umcdiscipleship.org/resources/new-membership-vows-and-ritual-revised-and-corrected (accessed March 21, 2018).
2. http://www.cyberhymnal.org/htm/w/q/wqsimhis.htm (accessed September 28, 2011).
3. Will Willimon, *United Methodist Beliefs* (Louisville: Westminster John Knox, 2007), 13.
4. Charles Wesley, "Spirit of Faith, Come Down," in *The United Methodist Hymnal* (Nashville: The United Methodist Publishing House, 1989), 332.
5. John Wesley, quoted in *The Quotable Mr. Wesley*, ed. W. Stephen Gunter (Atlanta: Candler School of Theology, 1999), 12.
6. Brian D. McLaren, *More Ready Than You Realize* (Grand Rapids: Zondervan, 2002), 14.
7. Mark Mittelberg, *Building a Contagious Church* (Grand Rapids: Zondervan, 2000), 247-322.
8. John Wesley, quoted in *The Quotable Mr. Wesley*, ed. W. Stephen Gunter (Atlanta: Candler School of Theology, 1999), 42.
9. Stephen Verney, *Fire in Coventry* (Westwood, N.J.: Revell, 1964), 76-77.
10. J. Ellsworth Kalas, *Our First Song: Evangelism in the Hymns of Charles Wesley* (Nashville: Discipleship Resources, 1984), 31.
11. Charles Wesley, "O for a Thousand Tongues to Sing," in *The United Methodist Hymnal* (Nashville: The United Methodist Publishing House, 1989), 57.
12. Charles Wesley, "A Charge to Keep I Have," in *The United Methodist Hymnal* (Nashville: The United Methodist Publishing House, 1989), 413.

Appendix

1. John Wesley, "Letter to Dr. Conyers Middleton," 1749, http://wesley.nnu.edu/john-wesley/the-letters-of-john-wesley/wesleys-letters-1749/ (accessed March 21, 2018).
2. Ibid.

MY NOTES

My Notes